THE GENERAL AND I

Published by Maverick House Publishers

Maverick House, Main Street, Dunshaughlin, Co. Meath, Ireland.
Maverick House SE Asia, 440 Sukhumvit Road, Klongton, Klongtoey,
Bangkok 10110, Thailand.

info@maverickhouse.com
http://www.maverickhouse.com

ISBN: 1-905379-09-9
978-1-905379-09-5

5 4 3 2

The paper used in this book comes from wood pulp of managed forests.
For every tree felled at least one tree is planted, thereby renewing
natural resources.

A CIP catalogue record for this book is available from the British
Library.

Author's note: Italicised names have been changed to ensure privacy.

The General and I

The Untold Story of Martin Cahill's Hotdog Wars

by Wolfgang Eulitz

DEDICATION

I would like to dedicate this book to Sophia, my daughter.

ACKNOWLEDGEMENTS

I would like to thank Brian Higgins and Denise Ruth for their constructive criticism whilst reading my early drafts.

I would especially like to thank Alice Healy for her inspiration.

— PROLOGUE —

28 January 1993

I pushed open the front door and stepped into the hallway. The volume on the television set seemed to be lower than I remembered and Katja, not that she had reason to, didn't call out to confirm who it was, the way people often do. I sensed something uncanny; maybe a primitive instinct was warning me that things were not as they should be. The wrong kind of silence was shrouding the hallway. I pushed the door closed with my free hand and turned around.

A man wearing a black balaclava sprang from the doorway of the downstairs sitting room. At the end of his outstretched hands he held a gun, which he now aimed directly at my head. Standing in the hallway, with his legs spread apart, he looked like an evil 007 agent, but his stature was that of late teens.

For a moment I thought he might have been a friend of a friend playing a practical joke—a sick kind of joke under the circumstances. I didn't recognise the physique. Through the cut out sockets of his balaclava, his black eyes bore into my own. They were cruel and hollow.

'Get in there and lie down!' he shouted in a harsh Dublin dialect, using the gun as a pointer. I obeyed, slowly at first, bewildered, still holding the milk carton and video in my hands. A second gunman; he was older and stockier, hurried down the stairs towards the hallway as if he'd been waiting to do so on cue. He had a thicker double-barrelled gun in his hand. It was probably a sawn off shotgun. He didn't speak.

As I entered the sitting room I saw Katja lying face down on the black leather couch. She had been gagged and blindfolded and her hands were tied behind her back. Apart from that she seemed to be unharmed. I put the milk and the video on the grey short-pile carpet and lay down on my stomach as if preparing to do a press up.

'Come on, hurry up!' the teenage thug barked. He was standing a few feet behind me; a quick glance revealed that his gun was still aimed at my body. As soon as I lay flat on the floor my legs were tightly bound with washing line and my wrists were tied behind my back. The twine was so tightly bound that it cut into my skin. A scarf was used to gag my mouth and my black leather jacket was thrown over my head to blindfold me.

'What's your name?' the teenage thug demanded.

'Wolfgang,' was my muffled reply. The scarf obstruction was yanked down from my mouth.

'What?'

'Wolfgang,' I repeated.

'Anyone else coming here tonight?'

'No.'

'You sure?'

'I don't think so,' I replied. The gag was replaced.

'You anything in your pockets?'

Once again I was unable to answer properly through the gag. A hand went into my trouser pocket and about £100 and my provisional driving licence were removed.

'What's his name?' the gunman shouted at Katja.

'Wolfgang,' Katja replied quietly.

The teenage thug stepped out of the room. I heard whispers. The older thug must have been higher up the food chain and didn't want to be recognised. The younger thug came back into the sitting room and I heard his breathing. The solid barrel of a gun was pushed against the back of my head.

'Where's the money hidden?' he barked. The gag was pulled away from my mouth.

'There is no money in the house.'

'Don't lie to me,' he said and pushed the gun harder against my skull. It was scary as hell knowing the hard metal sticking into my head was the barrel of a loaded gun. I feared a mistake could set it off and I tried to prepare myself for that possibility, in part by seizing up.

'I swear there's no money,' I said in monotone.

'There was money here before.'

'It's all gone.'

'I thought you'd a restaurant.'

'It was burnt out eight weeks ago.'

There followed an inane bout of laughter from both thugs. The gun withdrew from the back of my head. I took the laughter as an admission of guilt for both the restaurant fire and the £1,000 worth of bagged change that had mysteriously vanished from my room some months before. This was a hell of a way to solve those crimes. So now they were looking for more money and assumed it was hidden somewhere in the house. Maybe that was how these thugs got paid.

The television stayed on. It was strange to hear. They were sounds from a safe place. The words bounced off me. I could have listened all night long and not absorbed a single word. What little hope I first had that this was only an aggressive house burglary faded altogether. These thugs were here for more than just money. These thugs belonged to Martin Cahill, alias 'The General'.

— CHAPTER ONE —

It was April 1987. I was 23 years of age and broke, but I had an idea how I might make some money.

With £200 borrowed from my mother, I purchased the skeletal frame of an old horse box and eight sheets of half-inch marine plywood. I was going to build a food stall and sell portions of Pasta Bolognese covered in melted cheese at football matches and outdoor concerts.

My class mate and mentor, Jens, was going to help me build it. He had the know how and he had the tools.

Every morning I hitchhiked from Booterstown Bird Sanctuary, near where I lived, and made my way along the coast to Monkstown village. To improve my chances of actually getting a lift, I'd press the stop button at the first set of traffic lights I came across, wait for all the cars to stop, and then ask each driver in turn if they were going my way. Upon arrival, I'd get straight to work on my food stall in the back-yard of a house which Jens's parents had bought as an investment. My deal with Jens was that I'd help him gut his parents' property if he helped me build my food stall.

A few days later I hitchhiked to the Victor Hotel on Rochestown Avenue to meet a man about a gas cooker. He was heavy set, wore a shiny suit and spoke with a northern accent.

'It's called a wok, and it's ideal for what you want to do.'

We walked out of the lounge to the back of his big car. I don't know why he insisted on meeting me inside the plush hotel. He opened up the boot of his car and I saw the rusty old wok he was referring to. It looked like the skeleton of a cooker plundered from a skip. I'd always thought a wok was a bowl-shaped frying pan.

'It came out of a Chinese last week,' he said turning one of the knobs, as if this action proved the wokasaurus was still in good working order.

I was a little shocked and speechless.

'Needs some elbow grease; no problem for a hard working young business man like yourself,' he said.

I couldn't believe he wanted £350 for it.

'I've one more cooker I need to look at,' I said, and got the hell out of there. The cooker could wait.

About three weeks later, when my food stall still looked like a big wooden box with a V-shaped roof, Jens suggested I take it to Lansdowne Road, where Ireland was due to play Brazil in a friendly football match.

'I haven't got everything I need to sell Pasta Bolognese,' I said.

'Why not sell hot dogs instead—you only need hot water, frankfurters and bread rolls,' Jens replied.

'The stand won't be painted in time. It looks awful.'

'People won't care. It'll be a good way for you to get started.'

Jens was good at casting my doubts aside, so with a bit of cajoling, I went to my local shop and bought a *Buy and Sell* magazine to check out used cars. Later that day I purchased a yellow Peugeot 104 with another £300 I borrowed from my mother. I didn't have money to insure the car and couldn't tap my source for more, so I was lucky the old tax and insurance disks were still displayed on the windscreen. Next, I needed frankfurters and bread rolls.

Jens suggested I go to Hicks Butchers in Sallynoggin. They made the best frankfurters because the proprietor and his sons had learnt their trade in Germany. Purdy's Kitchen in Sandymount made the best bread rolls. The baker there told me he only used French flour, which was pure, because Irish flour contained too many additives. I painted up a sign which read 'Wolfie's unfinished hot dog stand' and bought a two-ring camping gas cooker in a local hardware shop.

When I arrived outside Lansdowne Road, I was full of enthusiasm and confidence. I bided my time stirring frankfurters with my metal tongs and cutting bread rolls as I waited for the game to end and the crowds to emerge.

There was a thunderous eruption from the crowd in the 33rd minute of the match when Liam Brady performed a brilliant fast-footed manoeuvre, outwitting the otherwise impregnable Brazilian defence. Before I knew it the game was over, 1-0, and the fans were released from the sport's colosseum.

The crowds streamed past my hatch for 20 minutes during which time I sold 12 hot dogs. I don't think anybody got the connection between 'Wolfie's unfinished hot dog stand' and 'Schubert's unfinished symphony', but that didn't matter. During the minor rush my tongs slipped out of my hand and fell into the boiling water. I had to fish out the remaining frankfurters using two forks. Sales were bad, and not because my metal tongs went absent without leave.

People didn't seem to trust frankfurters. Even the way they said it—BOILED SAUSAGES—made the product sound unappetizing. Did these people not know about frankfurters? That's how you make a frankfurter: you boil it in water for 5-10 minutes, remove it with a tongs, preferably non-heat retaining, and enjoy the crisp bite as the pork flavour pops in your mouth.

I was accustomed to frankfurters. I had grown up with them, but then I had a German upbringing, and thankfully there was a place in Dublin called Magill's Delicatessen that had always stocked them.

Maybe the reason for my poor sales was that people didn't trust the brown wooden box I was selling my hot dogs from. Things would improve, I told myself, once I painted the stand.

* * *

As soon as the colours went on—orange roof, yellow and orange sides—the neighbours began to complain. The problem with living in rented accommodation during the 1980s was that you could be treated like a second class citizen, because neighbours could put pressure on the landlord to evict you.

Nevertheless, I was ready for my next challenge. The following Saturday, Tina Turner played at the Royal Dublin Society (RDS). I arrived three hours before the gig was due to begin, only to find dozens of food stalls, some of them as big as juggernauts, already positioned near the venue. They were all open for business.

I was lucky mine was such a small unit; I could squeeze it in almost anywhere. Once again I was excited and full of confidence, although I did feel dwarfed by the food factories on either side of me, with their electric generators rumbling away loudly, pumping out fumes.

As the sound of Tina Turner thundered from the RDS, I watched a customer chew on one of my hot dogs. He chewed and chewed for a very long time but seemed to make little headway on the tough bread roll. Eventually he pulled the frankfurter out, ate it, and threw away the roll.

I looked at the discarded bread lying by the kerb— it wasn't good that the customer, a hungry lad, had trouble finishing his hot dog. Figuratively speaking, the hot dog should dissolve on impact once inside the mouth. I knew I had to improve my product. A lad from one of the other food stands came over to chat.

'Whatever you do, don't let the health catch you sleeping in the van,' he said.

I looked at the floor of my hot dog stand and cringed at the idea of lying on it. Dribbles of hot dog water mixed with shoe dirt and bread crumbs were smudged onto the roughened linoleum floor.

Cans of soft drink, boxes of chocolates, bags of bread rolls, the gas powered fridge containing the vacuum packed frankfurters, all combined to make the cold six by four foot floor an unappealing place of rest. And I was six foot two inches tall. My head would touch the scuff marks at the bottom of the door.

'You guys sleep in your food stalls?' I asked incredulously.

'On a long weekend you mightn't have any choice.'

'Really? All night long.'

'Yeah,' he said, shrugging his shoulders.

'I'll keep it in mind.'

'And don't give them your real name and address if they ask.'

He seemed to be a happy little fellow who spoke his truth and then ran back to his own food stall like a field mouse, scampering across a boreen.

* * *

Trade continued in dribs and drabs. I noticed that more people asked me for chocolate bars than hot dogs. With only a few pence profit on each chocolate bar, these sales were of little use to me. I didn't plan on being at this game for the next 40 years.

I made about 400% profit on a hot dog. Yet I wondered how many people would say, 'Ah go on so, give us a hot dog,' if I didn't sell chocolate bars.

I started to re-think my strategy when suddenly; a fireball ignited inside one of the juggernaut food kitchens next to mine. A deep fat fryer had caught fire along with the man standing in front of it. Fire extinguishers erupted all around him and the shaken man staggered through a thick mist of water vapour onto the street, before he was quickly driven away in a big northern registered car.

To my amazement only ten minutes passed by before the 'juggernaut' food kitchen was back in full production. One hour later the injured man himself was back on Lansdowne Road, to oversee his business.

Bandages covered his arms and hands and he had a big smile on his face. The hospital must have given him some very strong painkillers. I could see that the men involved in this game were hard men.

* * *

I knew the gig was nearly over because the best is always kept till last. The 'pre-empt the chaos people' had begun walking the streets. By the time Tina Turner had convinced us all that love had nothing at all to do with it, the roads were chock-a-block with thousands of bodies swept along like some unstoppable current of water.

The rush lasted half an hour, during which time I sold 24 hot dogs, and then business calmed to a light breeze.

What had gone wrong? I replayed the rush in my head. The hot dogs were not going out quick enough. There were too many condiments on my counter for customers to choose from and I saw many impatient people walk away from the back of the queue, while those being served spent an eternity deciding on what toppings they wanted. There was garlic mayonnaise, pickles, grated cheese and diced onions, shredded lettuce, sliced tomatoes, sliced gherkins, Sauer kraut and Tabasco sauce, as well as ketchup and mustard.

One girl in the queue suggested I only offer ketchup, mustard and coleslaw.

An hour later, with most of the people gone, I counted my money. I had grossed £36. At this rate I'd be 400 years old before I made my fortune. I turned off the gas, poured the leftover hot dog water into a nearby gutter, loosened the stabilising wheel and lifted the tow cup onto the tow bar of my Peugeot. The street was a mess, littered with thousands of gooey napkins, squashed cartons and leftover junk food. The rats from the nearby River Dodder would eat well that night.

* * *

Things were not going the way of my ambitious plans. What little money I had made selling hot dogs was lost on left-over stock. After the Tina Turner concert, I called into a friend's house and we had a hot dog party to get rid of what I hadn't sold. *Jesus, if I could only get customers to eat like that.* It was here that my new business venture idea really started to take shape, and I took the first steps towards a life more full of drama than I could ever have expected, or wanted.

At the party a guy called *Damien* suggested that I sell hot dogs in Leeson Street.

'It's always mad busy down there late at night,' he explained.

A busty blonde who worked as a lounge girl in Strings nightclub agreed with him. I could see their point. I figured that drunken people would devour hot dogs.

The only problem was that I didn't even know where Leeson Street was. In fact, when it came to Dublin town I was geographically illiterate, having grown up at the foot of the Dublin Mountains.

The next morning, I answered my front door to the dithery old landlord, who first apologised and then handed me my eviction notice.

* * *

With the inside of my hot dog stand now painted a bright white, I stocked up once again and drove into the city for my first attempt at serving the city's hungry late-night revellers. The bottle of gas that fed my cooker was now sitting inside a small wooden compartment situated on the triangular tow hitch. It felt safer knowing that the bottle of compressed gas was on the outside of the hot dog stand and not inches away from my groin.

I headed off towards Lesson Street on the first Friday of June, 1987. I pulled up onto a wide section of pavement located next to Hourican's Pub at the city end of the street.

As the local pubs regurgitated the last of their clientele, a few hungry stragglers spotted me and bought a hot dog for the road.

'Great idea,' one man said, 'but what are you doing down here? You should be up there, where all the action is.'

I couldn't see where he was pointing, so I stepped outside the hot dog stand and walked onto the street to get a better view. *Wow!* I couldn't believe it. About five hundred yards away from where I stood, thousands of bodies were congregated on footpaths, which appeared to extend far into the street.

Another straggler walked by, bought a hot dog and asked why I was down here, at the wrong end when all the people were up there.

'I know,' I replied with a self-critical sigh.

'These hot dogs are really good,' he said, trying to make amends, and walked on home.

I decided to stay where I was for the moment. I didn't fancy arriving 'cold' into a large crowd—at the very least I'd rather the crowd grew around me. An introspective pep talk was in order. No unskilled fortune ever came easy.

At 3 a.m. I put everything that was hot onto the floor of the hot dog stand, lifted the tow-hitch onto the tow bar of my car and drove up Leeson Street. I turned left and drove along a narrow road until I passed through an archway onto Pembroke Street. I decided that Pembroke Street was close enough to the crowds for now. I re-opened and sold another 50 hot dogs.

Two hours later, I packed up and drove home. Even as I turned left onto Leeson Street, dozens of people stood around. I guessed they were still waiting for taxis. I said to myself, "They must be starving!

My business mind starting going into overdrive. If I could make £70, positioned at the quiet end of Leeson Street and off the beaten track on Pembroke Street, what could I make here, where all the action was?

* * *

The following weekend at half past midnight, as I braved the final corner from Pembroke Street onto Leeson Street, the crowds swarmed towards my hot dog stand before I even came to a standstill. It was as though food aid had arrived for thousands of starving people. I had found my new pitch. I now had a large hot dog carved out of wood attached to the apex of my roof, advertising 'Wolfie's Hot Dogs'.

I didn't even have time to unhook the hot dog stand from the tow bar of my car. I disappeared through the back door, turned on the cooker, filled the pot with water and opened the hatch.

The ten minutes that followed, while I waited for the hot dogs to heat up, took forever. I got everything from, 'Wolfie how long will they be?' repeated over and over again to, 'I don't care if they're not cooked, I'll eat mine cold; I'm starving.'

Eventually, I was ready to roll and started to serve the queue as fast as I could. After an hour of intense hot dog making and selling there was a short lull and I was able to catch my breath and take stock.

I was on a high. I must have sold at least 48 hot dogs already. A rotund garda appeared before me like a bad vision and told me to clear off. I told him I couldn't because I'd already bought all the stock and that it would perish if I didn't sell it that weekend. He said it wasn't his problem. I showed him my trading licence but he replied that Leeson Street wasn't a designated trading area. I tried to argue that there was a serious need for food to soak up all the alcohol these people had consumed and were still consuming; but his answer was that the night clubs sold food.

'Yes, but expensive food,' I answered.

'That's not my problem either,' was his reply. 'You can't stay.'

'I really don't want to be on the dole,' I explained, but his look said 'piss off you little bollocks; you're not trading here.'

This debate of attrition went on for half an hour and then he walked away. I'd been polite the whole time. The garda mumbled something about wanting me gone by the time he came back but I didn't reply.

'I've never heard so much bullshit in all my life,' a lone customer said. He had been standing nearby watching the show.

'You have to believe in what you're saying,' I replied.

I didn't see the garda again that night. He may have seen me, but I didn't see him. I think that's important for the boys in blue; not to be seen losing face.

I soon got into the swing of things and learned my trade. Using a frying pan, I toasted the bread rolls when time allowed. This made the hot dog taste crispier and therefore easier to eat. A couple of customers even bought two hot dogs in succession. Putting coleslaw on a hot dog was innovative, and those who tried it seemed to like it. I no longer sold chocolate bars. If they're hungry, let them eat hot dogs.

At 5 a.m. I packed up the hot dog stand and decided to clean all the fallen napkins from the street. I figured that if it looked like a flock of large birds had been defecating on Lesson Street all night long and the office basements had gooey coleslaw napkins strewn all over their steps, it would only be a matter of time before a mightier hand of the law would sweep me away.

At 5.30 a.m. I went home to bed. I had sold over 100 hot dogs and it felt good. The following night I came even better prepared and grossed £150. A few days later I asked my baker to make the next batch of bread rolls lighter. I still wanted the same sized bread rolls; just lighter. This would make them easier to eat, and the easier they are to eat, the more likely you are to buy a second one.

Even though things were starting to pick up with the hot dog stand, I was still evicted, so a couple of weeks later, on a miserable Tuesday morning, I moved into a dingy little bedsit on Morehampton Road.

The room wasn't much bigger than my hot dog stand, and was even less well equipped. It had a ceramic wash hand basin as a kitchen sink and a two-ring camping gas cooker. This little hovel cost me the princely sum of £22 a week in rent. It wasn't worth it, but at least it was a place to return to every morning after a hard night's work.

I was still experimenting with the business and didn't want to limit myself to the one location. One afternoon I opened up my hot dog stand at the bottom of Grafton Street, where the Molly Malone statue now stands, in the hope of establishing 18 hours of continuous trade. But trading lasted all of ten minutes. You can tell when gardaí are bullshit proof.

I tried to argue that I was merely continuing the ancient Dublin tradition of street trading, but I guess a statue symbolising that part of our culture is preferable to the real thing, and I was moved on.

That June, U2 played Croke Park. At midday I found a place to park on Drumcondra Road as close to the nucleus of the atom as the gardaí would allow. The hours passed; people walked by, some bought hot dogs. A hardened youth walked up and forced himself over my counter, aggressive and fast, and grabbed a wad of paper money lying on the lower shelf. I held onto the thug for as long as I could, but slowly, finger by finger, I lost my grip. He was like a bar of soap. I shouted after him. In the struggle, two notes dropped from his hand onto the floor of the hot dog stand, a five and a ten were saved. When the thug was 20 feet away from the hot dog stand a garda caught hold of him.

'Tell the copper it's not him or we'll burn your fuckin' stand to the fuckin' ground,' the thug's accomplice growled menacingly. He was standing in front of the hatch and looked me straight in the eyes.

The garda looked to me for confirmation that he had the right person.

'Your friend took £40 from my till. I want it back,' I calmly stated, though the blood was racing through my veins.

'I've no money on me. Tell the copper it's not him. We'll find out where you live.'

The garda and the thug were now both looking in my direction, awaiting confirmation. I avoided eye contact.

'I'd say your friend has previous convictions. He'll get three to five years for this. I want my £40 back.'

There was a brief stand-off.

To my surprise the accomplice dug deep into his trouser pocket and withdrew £25.

'That's all I have,' he said, and offered me the bribe.

I took the money and waved 'nay' to the garda. A member of the public handed me a £10 note he said the thug dropped as he tried to make his getaway. I picked up the ten and five from the floor. The garda let the thief go and as he walked past, I apologised and explained.

'His mate threatened to burn me out, I'm hardly camouflaged and I got my money back.'

He lifted his head in disappointment, and dropped it in understanding.

As evening approached and twilight enveloped the city, the street emptied quite suddenly and I began to worry about those thugs again. Five minutes later I was packed up and on my way to a more familiar Leeson Street.

I was three hours early but felt that there was no point in my going home, so I opened up for trade. With the masses from the U2 gig still dispersing throughout the city I sold another 40 hot dogs before my normal late night trade began.

By 6 a.m. I was up over £250, but 20 hours of solid slog had left me wrecked. At that point, I decided that it wasn't worth killing myself doing sessions like that. Even as I drove the short distance to my bedsit on Morehampton Road, I found myself nodding off at the wheel and jerking back to life again on the wrong side of the road. It was lucky for me no one else was using the road at that time. When I eventually got to my flat I was ready to drop, and I fell into bed fully clothed.

* * *

I was sleeping off my exhaustion, but in my dreams there was a ringing in my head and it wouldn't go away, no matter what I did or where I went. I woke up, and the ringing was still there. It was coming from outside, probably a house alarm. I was too tired to get up and see – and what difference would it make anyway? I turned sideways and put the pillow over my ear, but the clinging and the clanging burrowed through the feathers into my head like a jack hammer. *Why the fuck doesn't someone turn that fucking alarm off?*

The loud ringing continued, and being a light sleeper, I couldn't doze off again. It was Sunday morning—this painful noise could continue all the way into Monday morning. A brain rage was brewing. *I need my fucking sleep.*

At 11.30 a.m. I tore myself out of bed like a possessed demon and stormed out of my bedsit. The alarm for the business school next door was ringing at Fire Brigade level. The area around the front of the school was deserted. I studied the terrain and walked over to the main entrance. The porch was the size of a small shed and within a moment I had climbed onto it and was kneeling in front of the alarm box.

The ringing was now hurting my ears. Without further delay, not wanting to stay long in this conspicuous position, I took a Swiss army knife out of my coat pocket and cut a cable just visible behind the plastic box covering the alarm unit. The ringing stopped, though not in my head. Across the street, people standing at a bus stop looked on and I got the impression that they silently agreed. Some applause wouldn't go amiss, I thought to myself. I climbed down from the porch; it was trickier than climbing up, and went back to my bedsit.

As far as I was concerned, my sleep was going to become increasingly important if I was going to make my new business a success.

— CHAPTER TWO —

The following Friday night, after only an hour's trade, I saw two gardaí walk towards my hot dog stand. They walked the walk of men who meant business. They were not interested in what I had to say about the stock or not wanting to be on the dole. They simply informed me that a tow truck was already on its way. The fee for reclaiming my hot dog stand from the car pound would be £150 and everything inside the food stall, including all my takings, would be confiscated. That would have left a nasty little dent in my financial situation. Customers in the queue were not happy and pleaded with the gardaí to let me make them just one more hot dog, but the two men stood firm.

Naïve and alone, I wasn't going to call their bluff, so I packed up and went home, relieved I had gotten away. But the fighter in me knew I had to get back onto Leeson Street.

I had no doubt that it was the night clubs who had pulled the necessary strings; such was their relationship with the gardaí. I wasn't able to offer them Christmas crates of wine. All I could offer was a hot dog with the works. The clubs obviously thought I was affecting their business. Who was going to pay £20 for a steak sandwich when I, the Michael O'Leary of Leeson Street, was selling tasty hot dogs for only £1? I was Ryanair with a smile.

A few days later I was walking home from the city centre. It was a drizzling overcast day and I was mulling over what I should do next as regards my lack of trading options. My legs began to ache as I came to a crossroads. Straight ahead lay a one mile trek to my bedsit, a right hand turn led to Harcourt Terrace Garda Station, and one final chat to plead my case. It was tempting to go home, play guitar and work on a couple of songs I'd written.

Calling into the Garda Station was the last item on my list of things to do and one I had been putting off all day long. I wanted to speak to a garda about trading on Leeson Street and to point out all the advantages of me doing so. Surely it was fair to feed drunken people when they most needed soakage, and without ripping them off when doing so. I wanted to argue that I was providing a much needed service and making a living for myself at the same time—keeping me off the dole. It was more or less the same regurgitated monologue I'd been using all along. What else could I say to them? There was nowhere within a mile of Leeson Street that sold fast food late at night, so I wasn't taking away business from any fixed premises.

Owners of these fixed premises would argue that while I had almost no running costs, they were paying rent, rates, insurance and wages. There were, of course, the nightclubs, but everyone knew the nightclubs were only interested in selling wine. Officially the nightclubs were restaurants with wine licences and dance licences but their primary function was selling overpriced wine.

Leeson Street didn't want to sell beer.

In those days pubs sold beer until 11.30 p.m., one or two legitimate nightclubs in the city, like The Pink Elephant, sold beer until 2 a.m. and then there was Leeson Street, to cater for the hardened socialite. The nightclubs knew that by three or four in the morning the most an intoxicated person might be expected to drink was one or two beers—the profit on a beer was £2 or £3; the profit on a bottle of wine was £20 or £30.

The rank and file garda opened the public hatch and asked, with a friendly country smile, what he could do for me. I explained my predicament and asked to speak with the highest-ranking officer in the station. He informed me that he was currently the highest-ranking garda in the station. Probably the only garda in the station. We spoke for ten minutes, with me making many points. He listened and took notes, which at the time I put down to courtesy, and then told me that he would have a word with the inspector. I thanked him for listening, but I didn't hold out much hope. Why would the gardaí suddenly change their minds? Why did I even bother making the detour? The walk home was long and depressing. The next day I signed on the dole.

I had an idea for a book and I contemplated starting a career in writing science fiction, but luckily for science fiction readers, I was forced to put my literary ideas on hold. I got a phone call from the same friendly garda in Harcourt Terrace Garda Station and was told that I could trade on Leeson Street after all. I couldn't believe my luck. I thanked him for his help, signed off the dole, and began my Leeson Street experience in earnest. As it turned out, the gardaí were a piece of cake compared to the other troubles I would later encounter.

* * *

By the summer of 1988, I was surfing on the wave of my first financial success and working six nights a week. I had vacated my dingy little bedsit on Morehampton Road, where the landlord held back my deposit because of wear and tear to the cheap bit of carpet running 10 feet from the front door to my bed. I in turn didn't pay the final electricity bill, which was still in his name.

I had changed my frankfurter suppliers because Hicks could no longer meet my increasing order. My new bread supplier, O'Leary's Bakeries, made all the bread rolls the same size, incredibly light weight, and delivered them to my door. The German Salami Company made every frankfurter 5-inches long, vacuum packed 30 in each bag, and also delivered them to my door. This new service gave me an extra hour and a half in bed every afternoon and my raw hot dog cost was reduced by 30%.

I was now living in the less conservative flat-land of Rathmines in south Dublin, with three lads I'd acquainted on Leeson Street. The owner of our Georgian building had taken a large room and prostituted it into four cubby-holes, an open plan kitchen-cum-sitting room and squeezed in a tiny toilet-cum-shower we tried not to use. The rent was £18 a week and I got no grief from the young entrepreneur landlord.

'I don't care what you do for a living, as long as you pay your rent,' he said.

* * *

I spent very little time in my shoebox bedroom, except to sleep for a few hours, being too busy most of the time to do anything else. I arrived most nights on Leeson Street—the growing heart of Dublin's very late nightlife—at 10 p.m. This secured me parking and two hours of internal preparations. Bread rolls needed to be sliced open and stacked and kitchen towels separated and piled for when the crowds arrived.

I discovered that speed was the key to success. At midnight, the giant stage that was Leeson Street came alive with thousands of people in heat. They hovered like birds around a fishing trawler. Nowhere in Dublin did so many people congregate so late on one street. It was 'Last Chance Avenue' where you could obtain alcohol and hope to meet someone for casual sex. And because the nightclubs didn't charge an entrance fee, I was guaranteed a steady stream of horny, hungry people, who yo-yoed from basement to basement looking for action. At a dozen nightclub entrances, bouncers shadowboxed and played judge and jury as to who gained access to their late night dens. Theirs was a verdict determined by looks, familiarity, and wallet size.

* * *

I was anticipating trouble with the gardaí, despite my earlier reprieve. They had threatened to close me before; and I had fought back with logic and patience. But after months of trading, one particular garda became determined to close me down.

He had let me trade for a year, as he put it. However, three recently arrived food stalls were, in his opinion, turning the street into a carnival. I wondered if that 'carnival' included the 12 nightclubs. Other traders had seen the wisdom in what I was doing and were eager to cash in. I had no objections to their presence because they accepted and respected mine. Once they had established their own pitch, these guys were actually okay and I got on well with them. They never tried to muscle me out, even though they knew I was alone.

The garda had told me about his concerns the night before—to give me a chance to sell what stock I had left. But I refused to leave and I arrived fully stocked the next night.

The serving hatch of my hot dog stand was now facing the street, and I quickly got used to the sights and sounds of the night. At my pitch, there wasn't much that could have shocked or surprised me.

In the midst of this drunken madness, the queue of revellers always grew and my trade began to flourish.

'Give us a couple of hot dogs with the works and where'd you get a woman around here?'

'For cash or free?' I asked as I placed a toasted bread roll on a sheet of kitchen towel held in the palm of my left hand. Using a plastic tongs, I pulled a five-inch frankfurter from a pot of boiling water beneath the counter. I had by this stage replaced the two-ring camping gas cooker with a more powerful three-ring wrought iron cooker. There were two pots on the boil at all times, sitting on either side of a large frying pan. While one pot was good to go, the other one heated a fresh batch of frankfurters.

'Free.'

'They're all around you gagging for it; just pour enough leg-opener into any one of them and look like you're interested.'

'Interested in what?'

'Their conversation.'

I dropped the sausage into the open bread roll and dressed it with ketchup, mustard and coleslaw. Moments later the second one was made. The money disappeared into a large plastic tub sitting next to a pillar of kitchen towels.

On my left, a student dressed in 'black tie' had fallen asleep on the wide granite doorstep of a Georgian Building. The side of his head lay cradled against the wrought iron railing, which saved him from falling into the basement. His arms and legs lay limp on the cold stone. He looked dead. Steam began to rise from his crotch. It was a sign of life. A wet circle formed and got bigger. Finally his entire leg was drenched beyond capacity and a stream of urine formed and meandered towards the footpath. At first a wry smile formed on the student's inebriated face, but his expression turned into a frown as the liquid cooled.

'Wine's expensive and the muff's not guaranteed,' my customer complained.

'Nothing's guaranteed on this street except the hot dogs,' I said and prepared several more in advance.

In this fast moving game you had to tell the customer what dressing they wanted to avoid losing those at the back of an impatient, hungry queue. I had become a high precision hot dog making machine. It could take an intoxicated man three long minutes to decide between ketchup, mustard and coleslaw. So you can imagine my frustration, when in the early days, I offered a delicatessen of condiments.

'One with the works?' I said, prompting a hungry man. He was swaying a little and staring at the coleslaw bucket.

'Yeah, give me one and don't poison me. What's that white stuff in the grey bucket?' he asked.

'Coleslaw, it's good for you, that'll be £1.'

I took the note and handed over the hot dog. The man, who looked like an ogre in a suit, pushed half the hot dog into his cave-like mouth. A dollop of creamy coleslaw ran down the side of his face and fell onto his dark jacket. There it rested like bird droppings. As he munched, his eye strained to glimpse the stain and his expression said it all.

'This is going to be a problem with the wife, which I will deal with tomorrow. For now I eat.'

On the other side of the granite steps a debutante attended to her partner as he sat leaning, eyes shut blissfully, against the wall of the old building. What was he thinking? Was he on drugs? From the expression on his face he was happy about something. The young man's jacket lay strewn across his lower body and covered most of the debutante's right arm.

I looked a little closer—could it be—in full view of anyone who cared to notice—even if it was midnight in this jungle of hormones—the centre of the black jacket rose and fell like a panting heartbeat.

'I'll have three please, with none of that white stuff, and "Heavy on the miracle whip Harry," another customer laughed.

'No, never heard that one before,' I lied politely. Why do people always think they're the first to deliver a one-liner—especially one that's been broadcast on national television twenty times a day?

Across the street, a scraggy young man ripped away the bright red shirt clinging to his body and flung it to the ground in frustrated anger. His posture stiffened, eyes narrowed, and his arm and finger extended like a rifle taking aim. Girls sniggered as he hopped about like a frightened squirrel dodging a poisonous snake. From his small mouth came a hail of badly spoken threats like, 'Cum on I'll fuckin' burst ye,' and, 'Yis are all fuckin' wankers'.

But the bouncers he was angry with only laughed and invited every challenge he made. He continued to step erratically and shout and finger point. People stopped walking and turned to watch with humour as he declared that he was with the IRA and that he'd be back to, 'BURN THE FUCKIN' PLACE DOWN'—a threat the bouncers received at least a dozen times a week. He certainly wasn't getting into any nightclubs after that performance.

'What are they like?' a potential customer asked an eating customer.

'This white gear is pure magic, give me another one,' the ogre demanded.

There were now numerous streaks of coleslaw on his dark suit.

'I'll have two of those please, but don't give me any of that white stuff,' one man said.

'I fancy a shag and I haven't got the patience for this crap,' another man said.

'Try Fitzwilliam Square, it'll work out about the same.' I indicated the route to take for a sure thing, talk-free shag.

A bottle of basic plonk retailed at £25 in the nightclubs. Straight sex retailed at £25 on the square, if you weren't too fussy. After some consideration, one man said he was going for a walk and another man conceded he was going home to 'the Wife'.

Suddenly the scraggy young man lunged at one of the bouncers. He fought like a woman, his swings uncoordinated. Three of his friends materialised from the crowd and joined in kicking and punching. Where the hell did they come from? Gentlemen pulled their women to safety. The bouncers were in trouble. Entertainment while you ate; but trouble like this attracted the gardaí, who could swiftly shut down the street and turn off the money taps.

'Excuse me, that'll be £5 please,' I said.

'Oh yeah, there you go,' the customer said, still watching the fracas.

Within seconds a vigilante army of 22 bouncers descended upon the vicious brawl. It was quickly subdued and the scraggy man and his friends fled, shirts torn, bruised and bloodied. 12 nightclubs in competition, but their physical unity made each individually invincible. The fiver disappeared into the big plastic tub beneath the counter.

A toothless misfit in tattered clothes appeared before me. I would only have recognised him by name, so I didn't know who he was. The few teeth he did have left in his mouth protruded crookedly and without order. His large eyes glazed over his dilated pupils and a wide smile pulled his face apart. He had mug-handle ears and scruffy hair—in essence, Shane MacGowan looked like shit.

I was perplexed by the presence of this ragged individual on Leeson Street. Surely he would have been refused entry to most of the nightclubs by now, and would therefore have gone home or fallen asleep somewhere. He bought a hotdog and walked back towards the one club that might still let him in; Suesey Street, named after Leeson Street's former name, which catered for Dublin's wilder artistes. It was only then that another customer told me who he was.

* * *

Leeson Street was an odd contradiction. The Rape Crisis Centre was located above Fanny Hill's nightclub, the Well Woman Clinic across the road from Legs. On Sunday mornings, yuppie mothers with stern faces brought their daughters to the clinic. Girls, who may have briefly submitted to the charms of a testosterone-driven prince the night before, now needed to expunge the previous night's promiscuity.

As I brushed the oily coleslaw-stained footpath with caustic soda mixed in warm water, I thought the girls left the clinic spiritually weakened and sad.

CHAPTER THREE

'Feed me Wolfie!' I recognised the voice. It was the 'fat man'. I liked 'fat man'—he held the hot dog eating record—nine with the works.

Situated where I was, among the late-night revellers, the working girls, the taxi men, the oddball characters and the graveyard shift gardaí, I got used to seeing all kinds of human behaviour. Leeson Street was a world in a microcosm, but as I was beginning to see, it was a strange world.

The gardaí arrived in numbers and attempted to shift a long line of double-parked taxis. Every time this happened I felt a surge of anxiety—I would be next. Taxi engines idled. The taxi snake was slow to move so licence plate numbers got scribbled into little black books as punishment. Personal details were given begrudgingly.

'Somewhere in the city houses are being broken into . . .' one taxi man argued. Everyone had their own style of bullshit for the gardaí.

One night a man wearing a long beige Mackintosh went crazy and began to attack the gardaí as they engaged the taxi drivers. He was an autistic man from

Drogheda who called everyone 'ye little chicken' and spent hours talking to the taxi drivers as they stood in line waiting for fares.

They in turn gave him spare change. Sometimes he would flash open his Colombo Mac and proudly reveal cans of beer squeezed into several worn-out pockets. He prided himself on being able to correlate car registrations with taxi plate numbers. He seemed to have dozens of them in his head—sometimes pushing everything else out. When he didn't spend nights in a police cell, he'd sleep for hours in the back of a bus using his free pass.

A small man in a well-pressed blue suit and a spaghetti load of stripes on his shoulder pad approached. It was the garda.

'I thought I told you yesterday not to come back.'

'Give us two with the works,' someone asked over the garda's head.

'This shop is now closed,' the garda turned to inform the customer. His attentions returned to me.

'Now; are you going to leave?'

'Garda, I have all my documentation,' I said confidently.

'You do not have permission to trade on this street.'

'I have a trading licence.'

'Does it say you can trade on Leeson Street?'

'It's what Dublin Corporation sold me to sell hot dogs in this city.'

I handed the garda the licence. He looked at it.

'Show me where it says you can sell hot dogs on Leeson Street?' he turned the licence towards me.

'It's for the city as a whole. No trading licence identifies an individual street.'

'I also have a health licence.'

I unstuck the A5 laminated card from behind me and handed it to the garda. He glanced at it briefly.

'This doesn't say you can trade on Leeson Street either.' *It's a health licence for a mobile food stall. Why would it identify a specific location?*

'I'm just showing you that my paperwork is in order, and here is my P60.'

'Why are you showing me all this stuff?'

'So you can see that I'm also paying tax,' I replied.

The garda held the papers in his hands, unsure what to do with them. I'd clearly made an effort to become legitimate on this illegitimate street. And for a moment I thought he might relent.

'Show me the permit that states you can trade on Leeson Street,' he finally demanded in that official civil service drone.

'You may as well ask to see my "Zonk".'

'Excuse me?'

'I know . . . there's no such a thing as a "Zonk", just as there's no such a thing as a permit which specifies where in the city I can sell hot dogs. You are asking me for something that doesn't exist. Dublin Corporation sold me that trading licence to sell hot dogs in Dublin City. I have given you all the documentation I could possibly possess. All I am doing is selling hot dogs for

£1, not a rip-off price, to intoxicated, hungry people who are a little better off having eaten something.'

I'd fired my verbal cannon. Last night he hadn't hung around to hear it, because he only called by to tell me not to come back.

'You do not have a permit to sell food on this street,' he replied adamantly.

'Please tell me where I can obtain such a permit?'

'That's not my job. I'll be back in one hour. I want you gone by then, or you WILL be arrested.'

He slammed the papers on the counter and marched away.

The taxi snake continued to move sluggishly; every taxi man blaming the one in front for the slow progress. Two gardaí were holding the Macintosh man down on the bonnet of their squad car while a third one tried to handcuff him. The man's face was red with fury as he shouted and spat indiscriminately. He now had a new red cut on his forehead.

'What did he want?' *Mick* asked, nodding in the direction of the recently departed garda.

'My balls with mustard,' I replied and shoved the useless documentation into my trouser pocket. The health licence was re-stuck to the white wooden surface behind me, in case the local health inspector made a late night appearance.

Mick was an angry, weather-beaten old man who spoke like an aristocrat and wore a long coat lined with newspapers. He told me once that his family were rich; but hadn't told me he'd drunk away his share of the family fortune. He did suggest that they had robbed him. Now he relied on their handouts.

Once, over a cup of tea, he re-lived his wild years—lying drunk on a hotel bedroom floor, covered in money and women, with an expensive bottle of champagne close to hand. The newspapers lining his coat were good insulation on cold nights, he told me.

I asked *Mick* to keep an eye on the hot dog stand.

'I need to make a phone call,' I said and ran across the road to a phone booth on the corner of Leeson Street and Hatch Street. Five minutes later I was back at my post. A group of men stood before me. They were speaking to each other in German.

'Such a wooden contraption would not be allowed in Germany.'

'I wouldn't touch the white stuff in the bucket; I bet he's been wanking into it all night long watching the girls go by.'

When they finished their mustard-only hot dogs one of them announced, 'Now, let's rip open some girls!'

It was at that point I asked in fluent German if any of them had ever been with an Irish girl before.

'Oh, you can speak German?' one asked.

'Indeed I can,' I replied. 'And if you carry on with that attitude, the only thing you'll be ripping open tonight is a packet of crisps.'

* * *

On television, I believe the amount of breast revealed by an interviewed entertainer is often proportionate with the decline of her career—not so on Leeson Street.

'Hi Wolfie,' said a seductive voice.

'Ah, my favourite cleavage,' I said. From my elevated station inside the hot dog stand I observed many of Dublin's finest cleavages, displayed using the latest in bra technology.

'You know what I want.'

'Indeed I do sweetie, but unfortunately I'm only licensed to sell hot dogs.'

With my left hand I held and pressured open a pre-cut toasted bread roll.

'You're incorrigible Wolfie,' she said with a smile.

'Only to you darling.'

I slid the unusually long frankfurter in between the open cheeks of the bread roll and covered it with coleslaw. Using the tips of my fingers, I placed the hot dog into the palm of her hand. She popped her mouth shut, lifted her eyes and smiled. Not a single drop of coleslaw spilt over her lips as she sauntered back into the hormone jungle.

* * *

At 3.30 a.m. the garda returned.

'I thought I told you to close this thing down.'

'I'm sorry, but I can't.'

'And why not?' he asked incredulously.

'Because it's my livelihood; without it I will be unemployed and on the dole.'

The garda moved closer, only inches separated our faces and he fixed me with his stare.

'Listen to me; you close this fucking hut right now or I will arrest you.'

There followed a tense moment. He meant business. I wasn't going to talk my way around his restricted logic.

From the corner of my eye I could see the journalist Eamon Dunphy walking briskly towards my hot dog stand. My call to the cavalry had not been in vain.

'Hey Eamo, how's it going?' someone called out.

'Do you understand what I am saying to you?' the garda asked.

'I do, Garda,' I said, and stood back.

Eamon approached, carrying a notebook in his hand.

'Good morning,' he said.

Earlier that evening I'd called into my mother's home to be fed and watered. My mother was living with Eamon at the time and as I sat there eating my *Rot Kraut und Rolladen*, he'd asked me how I was.

'Good, but I think I'm going to be closed down tonight,' I replied.

He asked me why and I told him about the garda and the warning from the night before. Eamon had told me to phone him if I was asked to close down. I said that this might happen at two or three o'clock in the morning.

'I don't care how late it is, you ring me.'

Now he had arrived just as the garda moved against me.

'Good morning,' the garda replied, momentarily taken aback.

'I believe you are closing this hot dog stand.'

'I am.' The garda immediately recognised the journalist.

'May I ask why?'

'Because he is trading in contravention of the street trading act.'

'Well if he is trading illegally, then you should close him.'

'That is what I am in the process of doing.'

'And will you then close all the night clubs that are trading illegally?' Eamon said with a sweeping view of Leeson Street. 'They are only licensed to sell wine until half past twelve, I believe, and it is now half past three,' he added.

'Now hold on one minute, my officers are dealing with those premises.'

'Are they really?'

'Yes they are.'

'Is that why there are punters going into them?'

'My officers . . .' the garda began but he was quickly closed down.

'Look behind you, Garda; people are still going into nightclubs.'

'I refuse to be drawn into . . .'

'Right over there,' Eamon cut in again and pointed to a group of people descending some stairs.

'As I said, my officers . . .'

'If you close this food stall and allow those nightclubs to stay open, I will expose you. And if I have to, I will go into every single nightclub and buy a bottle of wine to prove it.'

The two men stood face to face, but one set of eyes contained more conviction than the other. The garda went silent and then he went away.

It was a reprieve—the following weekend I received a parking ticket because the wheel of my car was parked more than six inches from the kerb. It was harassment in a way, but if that was the only harassment I was ever going to get I was laughing. The Garda would be the least of my worries.

The cooker burnt on full throttle all night long. Two powerful flames boiled large pots of water filled with frankfurters; the steam turned my work area into a pork-flavoured sauna. I was immune to the odour. The bright gas lamp hanging from the V-shaped ceiling generated more heat. The wooden hull of the hot dog stand surrounded me like a lagging jacket. During the three-hour rush, which continued from 2 a.m. until 5 a.m., people crowded the serving hatch to make my work place even hotter. I drank cans of fizzy orange to stay hydrated and wore a bandana to soak up the sweat. And not once did I ever need to step outside the hot dog stand to pee.

The emphasis on Leeson Street was on having a good time, but it was still the city centre and trouble lurked. You had to keep your wits about you.

Three men were heading my way one night and I didn't like the look of them. They were hardened youths, miffed at having been refused entrance by a nightclub, and they had anger to vent. I pulled a 12-inch jagged-edged knife from beneath my counter and held it at waist level.

'Here Bubbles! Look at the ponce in the horse box.'

I said nothing, picked up a bread roll and began to slice it slowly from end to end.

'I'll ram that knife up your fucking arse.'

A quick glance revealed that Bubbles was a nasty piece of work. I stayed calm and picked up another bread roll. The three men now stood before me.

'Give us three,' one of them demanded. A fight scar ran down the side of his face.

'That'll be three quid,' I said, and continued to slice bread rolls, tear sheets of kitchen towel and opened a new ketchup bottle to give the appearance of being busy and unconcerned. Scumbags can smell fear.

'What; you think we won't pay?'

I know you won't pay.

'They're cooking, it'll take a minute,' I replied.

I knew that if a customer made no attempt at all to retrieve money from his pockets while waiting for his hot dog to cook, there was a good chance that I wasn't going to get paid.

'Go fuck yourself,' he replied.

The three left without their hot dogs. The long knife remained visible until they were gone from the street—it was my passive psychological deterrent. Working on Leeson Street was like swimming in a lake knowing it contained at least a few hungry piranha.

* * *

Everyone paid for their hotdogs, even the police; a practice the bouncers found astonishing. Everyone that is, except Dublin's homeless. They didn't come to Leeson Street for the women or the wine. For them, like me, it was their place of business.

'Morning.'

'Hi John, you're early.'

'I couldn't sleep.'

'Are you having one?'

'I suppose I'll try one. Did you have a good night?'

'Not bad. Gardaí called by, cleared the place. I survived, but the man in the Mac got arrested again.'

'Good, might be a few bob left for me so—hand us out a bag and I'll get started.'

John was a chubby little man in his late fifties. I fed him hot dogs and gave him left over bread, which he in turn fed to the ducks on St Stephens Green pond or kept for himself. He often helped me clean up the street at the end of a night's session, which was always a blessing.

He had a round red face, skin like medium grade sandpaper and lived in the YMCA. Most mornings he walked the footpaths of the city with his eyes glued to the kerb and looked in between parked cars for fallen money.

Leeson Street was particularly lucrative. John had a vindictive streak, which he aimed at a local taxi man who also walked the street looking for lost money while waiting for the nightclubs to empty. One day John planted a shred of a £5 note under the wheel of a car, just to watch the taxi man's disappointed face after he'd reached down and picked it up. I think John felt he had an exclusive right to the fallen money on Leeson Street and that the taxi man had made enough cash being a taxi man. John didn't even like the man in the Mac finding money, because the autistic man already had his little 'chat for change' thing going with the taxi men.

Two taxi men were standing nearby eating a hot dog.

'So how's business?'

'Ah slow, you know yourself.'

Business was always slow for the taxi men, according to them, but lengthy queues of people told a truer story.

Eventually, when I myself was asked, and I didn't have twenty customers standing in line, I also moaned that business was slow. In the land of begrudgers, it didn't help to confess to success.

'I had a fare last night, you should've seen her. This bird had tits the size of watermelons,' the taxi man said cupping both hands above bouncing, pivoting elbows.

'What happened?'

'When we get to her place, she tells me she hasn't enough money—I'd done the third gear trick on her— but would I come in and we could work something out.' The taxi man's voice grew in volume as he climaxed his anecdote, but I had customers, so I would have to come back to him later.

'What kind of soup do you serve?' a woman asked. There were three men with her. *Hopefully they'll ask for hot dogs.* Selling 'cup-a-soup' turned out to be another daft idea I had to improve my menu.

'Chicken, beef and vegetable,' I replied. The menu was painted on the front of my hot dog stand, on either side of the hatch.

'I'll have a vegetable soup,' the girl asked giddily and then added, 'I don't eat dead pig,' before her friends took their turn.

'Chicken.'

'Chicken.'

'And I'll try the beef,' the last man ordered.

Cup-a-soup was a good product to have on a freezing cold, slow trade night, but a pain in the ass during a hot dog rush.

Opening the three 'cup a soup' containers and separating three paper cups, spooning the powder, using a second spoon for the vegetable soup on the instruction of the vegetarian and waiting for the water to boil in the big gas kettle took ages.

Then pouring the extremely hot water into each cup, stirring each cup individually and carefully handing the steaming hot cups to tipsy customers took even longer. Finally you had to close the containers, wash both spoons and deal change for each person. It took me five minutes to sell four cups of soup, and all this for a measly 30p a cup. I usually told people the soup machine was broken because on a busy night I could sell 20 hot dogs in the same time.

'This is delicious,' the yuppie hippie girl said cupping her hot soup.

'Yeah, but God only knows what's in it,' her posh companion replied.

'I'll tell you exactly what's in it,' I said.

And then, as I rested my elbows on the counter, I began to read out the ingredients. I don't know what possessed me to open my big mouth in the first place. I rifled through the E-100s and E-200s, the colourings and the flavourings. Then I got to extract of beef. As the 'B' word came out of my mouth I realised my error. Her expression exploded. She dropped the cup and spat and screamed. The footpath steamed.

'You told me this was vegetable soup.'

'I'm sorry but that's what it says on the tin,' I replied and showed her the big bold font: *Vegetable Soup*.

'You bastard, I haven't eaten meat in seven years!' she shouted, spat, and made towards me. Two of the men she was with held her back.

'I'm really sorry. I had no idea there was meat powder in this vegetable soup. How could I know? It says vegetable soup on the bloody container.'

'You made me eat meat you ignorant fucker. I haven't eaten meat in seven years.'

She kicked my hot dog stand one last time as the men pulled her away. There was no point offering her a free hot dog for the error. The woman continued complaining loudly and even said something about suing—an Irish pastime. The third man apologised and left. The next day I would paint over all the soup signs on the hot dog stand.

* * *

Suddenly I heard screaming. It was coming from one of the basements and getting louder. The bust of an obese woman appeared from the basement stairs of a nightclub. The large female was upset about something and fell about like a crazed hippo. Parked cars were dented as she collided with them. Sometimes she stalled, but the massive drunken woman continued to head in my direction. I stood up from my fold down seat to get a better view. Her size increased as she neared the hot dog stand. I panicked; she could turn me over and not notice.

'I'm closed,' I shouted, but to no avail. She screamed and wailed as if her entire family had been wiped out in a bomb blast. Using the internal support bars I vaulted myself over the counter and closed down the hatch. With just ten feet to go the human asteroid changed its trajectory and I was spared. That would have been my Armageddon.

A friendly taxi man then pulled up looking for an early morning snack.

'What's a third gear trick?' I asked him.

'The third gear trick is when a taxi man tips his index finger against the extras-button on the meter as he changes into third gear. It's worth 40p a tip.'

Today it is required by law that taxi meters are fixed at least six inches above the top of the gear stick for this very reason.

As I closed up, I noticed that the bottle of gas in the hot dog stand was empty, so I replaced it with a full one from the boot of my car. The gas felt heavier at 6.30 a.m., thankfully each bottle tended to last me about a month.

I rid the street of all discarded kitchen towels, packed up my hot dog stand and did a quick tally. I'd grossed over £400. There followed an eerie peace, disturbed only by stragglers falling out of nightclubs laughing. Then, as dawn approached, they fled like vampires from the oncoming sunrise.

— CHAPTER FOUR —

There was a public car park across the road from my
flat in Rathmines and this was where I kept my hot dog
stand. In there I had no neighbours to complain about
it bringing down the tone of the neighbourhood, but I
was vulnerable to a new kind of threat.

One evening the landlord burst into my flat to
tell me that my car was being broken into. I ran out
towards the car park and saw dozens of kids swarming
around my yellow Peugeot, and one was stuck inside
it. It looked as if the other kids had used his head as
a battering ram to break through the rear passenger
window and then left the trunk of his body lying flat
on trays of soft drinks. These he was now dissecting
and passing through the broken window to the other
kids. As I approached, and they realised that I was the
owner of the vehicle, the human flies dispersed. The
little boy's legs wiggled like a trapped insect. I grabbed
them and pulled him out of the car. Some gardaí arrived.
The little boy denied he'd been anywhere near my car.
I was surprised at the audacity of this minor.

'I know his parents', one garda began, 'they're on
the dole. If you take them to court you'll be lucky to

get five pence a week, and it will take you six months to get that judgment.'

I watched as the garda led the youngster to freedom.

'When they steal in my shop,' my landlord said, 'I take the little fuckers out back and give them a good hiding.'

I thought this was a bit harsh. Back then, I was still naïve enough to think that the way to deal with criminals was to go to the police.

* * *

Money was going missing from all our rooms. We were four suspects with no motives. It was very frustrating. There was *Joseph*, the funny chubby chef; *Jake*, who liked to live life in the slow lane and thought ambition was a capitalist swear word; some fellow from the country we hardly ever saw, and me.

I was taken off the suspect list because of how much money I was making selling hot dogs. *Jake* tended to hang around me most of the time like a loyal pet and the fellow from the country wasn't there enough to be guilty of anything. So only *Joseph* was left and that simply didn't make any sense. He just didn't have any badness in him.

One evening, a Canadian man, who had recently befriended us and lived in the flat above, called down for a chat. I was on my own and getting ready for Leeson Street: boxes of frankfurters, bags of bread rolls, two grey buckets full of coleslaw covered in cling film, and kilos of ketchup piled up on the sitting room floor awaiting transport to the hot dog stand. The Canadian seemed fascinated by the concept of Leeson Street and I could see him guesstimate the number of vacuum-packed frankfurters in the boxes, and how much money I was probably making.

I got an idea.

'I'm just going for a quick pee,' I said. When I returned to the sitting room, he said he had to, 'Go do some stuff,' and then he left the flat as quickly as he'd come into it.

'Okay, I'll see you tomorrow,' I replied.

As soon as he was gone, I checked the satchel leaning against the box of frankfurters. A minute earlier there had been £70 float in the bag, now there was only £35. *Case closed.* But when I went outside to confront the Canadian he was nowhere to be seen, and I was in a hurry to get to my parking space on Leeson Street. It would have to wait. Some other men had started to take notice of my booming trade, and were becoming a little too interested for my liking. I had hoped it was my imagination playing tricks, but I could have sworn I'd seen a few pairs of eyes watching me trade recently, and I doubted they were trying to decide what toppings they would like on their hot dogs.

I was open twenty minutes and busy slicing bread rolls, snapping sheets of kitchen towels and piling them up into a hexagonal tower. A face I recognised from somewhere approached.

It was one of the local business men.

'I wonder if we could meet for a chat tomorrow morning?' he said.

'Okay, what do you want to talk about?' I asked with polite intonation.

'I have a business proposition I'd like to discuss with you.'

'Where do you want to meet?'

'A hotel would be fine; let's say 11 o'clock,' he said and he named a hotel nearby to meet at.

'Okay, I'll see you there tomorrow at 11.'

I was kind of excited; even though getting up at 10.30 a.m. would be the equivalent of a normal person waking up in the middle of the night.

This guy was a successful business man; what could he possibly want from me?

First things first though. Late next morning, I called up to the Canadian's flat and knocked on the door. I was almost surprised that he answered it.

'Can I have a word with you?' I asked calmly as I stretched my eye lids apart. He led me into his barren room. I didn't waste any time and said my piece. He didn't deny his guilt and I could see that he was shaking and frightened. He looked a forlorn, pathetic figure of a man. I looked around his room: there was a tattered wooden chair and a single mattress lying on the floor—nothing else. The room didn't look that small anymore. Had he sold all the junk furniture that came with the flat? The place was filthy and there was no trace of his girlfriend. I realised that she might have left him. I took the £10 he had left in his possession and went away. I didn't know what else to say or do and I didn't want to add to his miserable existence by getting the police involved.

At 11 a.m. I met with the business man. We sat down at a table and he asked me whether I wanted tea or coffee.

'Tea would be fine,' I said. He motioned a passing member of staff.

'That's quite a profitable little business you have over there,' he said.

'I do alright,' I agreed.

'Leeson Street is a lot busier now than it was a few years ago,' he said, as if revealing something I didn't already know.

'I've improved my technique as well,' I replied.

'Do you know where you'd make even more money with your hot dog stand?'

I said nothing and watched his expression. With the exception of 42nd Street in New York, I couldn't imagine a more lucrative spot than my current pitch on Leeson Street.

'If you parked your hot dog stand on Hatch Street, you'd make a lot more money.'

I knew that wasn't true.

'I'm quite happy to stay where I am. You said you wanted to talk to me about a business proposition?'

It became apparent over the course of the next few minutes that this man just wanted to muscle in on my territory. He wasn't making any business propositions at all. In fact, he was subtly telling me that I should move my hot dog stand off Leeson Street, where it was now flourishing.

My heart sank. So this was the business meeting.

'We can do this the easy way or we can do this the hard way,' he said.

'And what exactly is that supposed to mean?' I asked.

'This meeting is over.'

He got up from the table and left the building. I stayed and finished my tea.

I was quite annoyed. I had forfeited my sleep for this. I certainly wasn't going to move my hot dog stand away from my established pitch. If I allowed myself be bullied once, there'd be no stopping the push.

I phoned Eamon Dunphy and explained what had happened. I don't know what Eamon said to him, but I never heard from that particular business man again.

The next day the Canadian went.

A few days later the landlord found a letter addressed to him hidden under the carpet of his old room. It was from a Scottish Court—they wanted him to answer a charge of theft from a youth hostel in Glasgow.

* * *

My business was bringing in a lot of money, but I was starting to feel the effects of the long and hectic work schedule.

The summer of 1989 began with the ultimate event: Frank Sinatra, Sammy Davis Jnr and Liza Minelli live in Lansdowne Road. I got a ticket to see the show from Eamon Dunphy.

At 8.00 p.m. I drove my hot dog stand to Leeson Street and walked to the gig.

Minelli cried a lot, Davis Jnr did the Jackson moonwalk and grabbed his 63-year-old crotch and Sinatra looked up at a passing airplane and said, 'Not when I'm on.'

During the encores I ran back to Leeson Street and began my night's work.

It was my third summer on Leeson Street and I'd cut myself a new lifeline on the palm of my hand slicing thousands of bread rolls a little too enthusiastically. Every afternoon I found myself waking up an hour later than the day before and by Friday I was sleeping until 5 p.m. Even after ten hours sleep I woke up feeling light-headed. A bowl of cornflakes and a cup of tea later my work day began.

I'd spend three hours making 40 kilos of coleslaw, cleaning out the hot dog stand and getting ready for the night ahead. I'd watch half an hour of MTV—they still played music in those days—and then I hit the road. Monday was my only day off.

I arrived as usual around 10.30 p.m. to ensure my pitch against the lamp post and a three meter gap to the boot of my car. The lamppost gave me some stability against a strong wind—the space in between the car and hot dog stand was for customers to queue and congregate.

Lately I had been driving more cautiously. With the hot dog stand pushing hard from behind, the brake pads swished wearily against the metal disc every time I slowed. Finding the time to get new brake pads would mean missing out on sleep I couldn't afford to lose. As I drove to work, the calm before the storm, Melanie's 'Left over wine' played on my car stereo and soothed my psyche for the night ahead.

The hookers waved as I trundled by, I waved back—in a way we all provided a little something for the hungry needs of late night Dublin. And we were all getting well paid for it.

It was interesting to see the different levels of class and taste in the prostitutes, and though I wondered what the difference in cost might be, I never tried to find out.

One night I had a chat with one of the girls. She was attractive. Not all of them were. She always wore the same green suit, was well groomed, bronze-tanned with long blonde hair drawn into a bun. She was the seductive airhostess. I watched as she stepped into a brand new Mercedes wearing a smile which suggested the recognition of an old friend. An hour later she reappeared, came over to my hot dog stand and ordered a hot dog; possibly to quell the bad taste in her mouth.

'You work long hours,' she said.

'I'm thinking of employing someone part-time so I might have a night off,' I replied.

'I'll work for you if you pay me £900 a night,' she replied, with a soft English accent—which city I couldn't tell. I was doing well, but not that well.

Another time, an old woman stood before me. She was small, wrinkled, and had no teeth. She looked mid-sixties; someone told me she was early forties, but no trace of her youth remained. The woman ordered a hot dog and handed me a moist £1 note. It was disgusting to touch, like wet paper pulled from a rancid trashcan. I looked away as she ate. Air funnelled through her mouth as her gums chewed noisily on the soft food. I tried not to listen. When she swallowed the last morsel the toothless old woman handed me 20 moist £1 notes, earned that night, and asked for a single twenty in return. I took the money, using index finger and thumb, and placed it in the corner of the money tub. I would deal with the diseased notes later.

The hideous old woman walked back towards Fitzwilliam Square to sell her mouth some more and I washed my hands in my semi-conical stainless-steel sink. Are the cheapest blow jobs really only £1 each?

* * *

Not everybody was nice and polite. Standing there alone, in full view of the drunken masses, I was an easy target for all sorts of people. Some wanted to intimidate me; others simply wanted to get in on the money I was making. Now, if anyone asked, I would say that business was 'slow'. It was the standard answer. If people knew how much money I was making there would be dozens of food stalls opened on the street within a week. As it was, there were still only three of them, and they only came on weekends.

I was up £100 by 1 a.m. It was going to be a good night, I could feel it. That is until a fat man, who himself owned a string of fashionable fast food outlets, tried turning me over by lifting the tow-hitch of my hot dog stand. It was a pre-meditated, drink-induced prank, accompanied by nasty laughter. He must have loosened the stabilizer bars at the back of the hot dog stand. A tidal wave of boiling hot water spewed across the shelf, drenching money, bread rolls, and pre-cut kitchen towels. I tried to hold everything in place and somehow get out of the death trap at the same time. It was my worst nightmare, being tipped over by a gang of drunken louts. After all, the hot dog stand was small and relatively lightweight. Inside the hot dog stand there were three burning flames, boiling pots of water and a grey bucket full of coleslaw to worry about. I could end up looking like a victim in a *Laurel and Hardy* movie.

My left hand was now scalded. Using the internal support bars I vaulted myself over the counter and Mr Fast Food, the laughing concept thief, ran away.

'I HOPE YOU'VE DAMAGED YOUR BACK, YOU FAT BASTARD!' I shouted. And then the burning pain on the back of my hand intensified. I removed a can of spray coolant from my first aid kit and sprayed away some of the pain. Ten minutes later the inside of the hot dog stand was restored and I was back in full production.

That same night, one of the bouncers, who fancied himself as a hard man entrepreneur, offered me a brown envelope with £3,000 to walk away from my 'hut', as he called it. *Was he for real?* The bouncer informed me that he was 'best buddies' with a senior garda and a bunch of other self-important wankers. He sang his subtle threats and I listened. He would have to sing a more convincing melody to coerce me out of my gold mine.

I was beginning to get pissed off by all of this less than welcome attention, but I thought I was well able to handle it, as long as I kept my head down and did my job. Business went from strength to strength.

During a serious rush, a hot dog was made every six seconds. These onslaughts from the public occurred all through the night and the object of the game, as I liked to think of it, was to not lose a single customer, no matter how long the queue.

I even considered pre-making hot dogs at an earlier time in the evening, wrapping them in tin foil and keeping them warm in a big steam oven. Sales would have doubled, but the quality of the hot dog would have suffered unacceptably. That idea stayed an idea.

The son of a well known bookmaker called by and handed me a bottle of nightclub champagne. I'd found his wallet the night before while cleaning the street. It contained £400 and a dozen credit cards. He was delighted.

Another guy called by and told me how much money I was lodging into my bank account each week. I found this news rather unsettling, because I was vulnerable to armed robbing thugs. He said he was friends with a member of staff at a bank. I would later have a word with the bank manager, who told me he'd have a word with the bank clerk. As long as everybody was communicating.

While I plied my trade, the antics on the street went on, and ranged from the strangely compelling, to the funny and harmless, to the outright dangerous. Sex-crazed youths, aggressive bouncers, and helpless drunks all played out scenes before my eyes. It was like watching a live wildlife documentary.

A man in his early twenties grabbed a ketchup bottle and aimed it at my head. He stood, legs apart, and tried to look like a special agent. I took hold of the bottle. His grip was strong, so I bent the nozzle 180 degrees. Believing he still had the upper hand, he squeezed the ketchup bottle hard. It took him a while before he realised that his own shirt was covered in red sauce.

A man, perhaps 25 years of age, wearing a white shirt and a dark jacket, stepped onto the granite steps of a nearby Georgian building and shouted,

'Is there anybody here who wants to have sex with me?'

Girls looked on and giggled: of course the rules of engagement wouldn't allow for a suitable girl to say yes and I don't think the gentleman would have wanted it so easily either. I could be wrong.

Every now and then, some big drunk fella would lean heavily against the counter and demand a burger and chips, or fish and chips, as if I were some kind of Tardis hot dog stand with a hidden kitchen.

'I only have tasty hot dogs.'

'Give us a couple of them so.'

I had recently split with my girlfriend, and while I was for the most part an innocent observer to the debauchery and hedonism of Leeson Street nightlife, I occasionally had a fling of my own. The street was constantly filled with young women out for a good time and I was a young man with a blossoming business, the focal point for the crowds spilling out of the nightclubs. More importantly, apart from the bouncers, I was the only sober man on the street.

This made the hot dog stand a magnet for women. In the early hours of the morning, after most of the madness had died down, a girl approached. She ate a hot dog and hung around to chat and smile and send her fertile message: Another hot dog groupie. I extinguished the gas at source and pulled down the hatch. She said her place was just around the corner and would I fancy a glass of wine. I said, 'Why not?'

We walked down a lane. Her home was swanky and white-washed. She led me straight to her bedroom and her top fell off. I yawned and kissed her mouth. Her breath smelt of foul alcohol. I must have reeked of sweaty pork. We lay on the ruffled bed. 'Play with me,' she said.

'I've just spent seven hours cooped up in a sauna from hell,' I replied.

A couple of minutes later I was done and made my excuses.

I walked back to the hot dog stand. Dawn had beaten me to her.

'Have you got any left?' a young man shouted as he ran down the street towards me.

'I might do, let me check.' I looked inside the pot.

The water had reduced significantly but was still warm. It was dark brown in colour and smelt of salty pork. There were six shrivelled hot dogs left floating. They looked like turds in a sewer.

'I'll have three with the works,' he called out from behind the serving hatch. I pushed out the hatch and daylight filled my workspace. The place was a mess. Everything looks better at night.

'I'll have three with the works,' he repeated.

'No problem. I might as well warn you, these are not my best specimens, so I'll put in a little extra.'

I placed two burst frankfurters into each bun, poured on the sauces and scraped out the last of the coleslaw from the grey bucket.

'There you go, that'll be £3.'

'Look, I've no cash left, but I've something in the boot of my car worth a lot more.' I gave him the hot dogs in trust. Tired and indifferent, I opened a can of

Fanta and watched as he ran across the street to his motor car. The boot went up. A minute later he was carrying something the size of a television set. I took a swig of fizzy orange.

'If you wait another hour, you can sell these to rush hour traffic.' He dropped a bundle of newspapers on my counter.

I looked at the date.

'Where the hell did you get these from?'

'My dad's high up in the paper,' he said as he ran back to the hot dogs in his car.

I did feel a little guilty about the girl in the swanky house; that is until the following night, when I saw her, arms draped around some other big guy, oblivious to me as she ordered two with the works. She seemed to be in high spirits, and so was I.

Most people were under no illusions that such late night encounters were anything more than one-night stands and all seemed fair in love and war. It was just harmless fun.

Some incidents I witnessed were far from harmless though, and served as a reminder that this was still the inner city, and that alcohol and testosterone were a dangerous mix.

I watched a man shadow some girls. When they stopped walking, he stood next to them, stared at them and grinned pathetically. I'd seen him do it before; that's what he did almost every weekend. He was a lost soul on the avenue of the desperate. With so many people congregating on the street, it might be a number of minutes before girls became aware he was weirding out on them.

Months later, when he'd weirded out a haughty glamour girl, an off duty bouncer but very much on-duty boyfriend chased him down to an unused basement. There he punched and kicked the teenager unconscious. Twenty minutes later an ambulance arrived and retrieved the teenager's dead body. I believe the attacker received many years imprisonment for his senseless crime.

At a quarter to six in the morning, the street went quiet. It was a sea of fallen kitchen towels drenched in coleslaw. I stared at the carnage in a trance.

A tall American bouncer was getting grief from a regular client he refused. *This late?* The 60-something man, who had a stomach bag he loved to show off at the hot dog stand, which I wish he didn't, continued to hurl abuse at the bouncer.

The bouncer stood still, turned his head left, studied the terrain, and then turned his head to the right. The street was deserted—I didn't count. Stomach bag man wouldn't shut up. Without warning the bouncer launched his fist into the old man's unsuspecting face. The impact sounded like a bunch of keys dropping to the ground. No defence was offered. The old man fell onto the pavement in a heap and the bouncer retreated into his nightclub. Then, as if a referee was counting down from ten, the old man struggled to his feet and walked away.

A Hiace van with a large trailer sped over the canal bridge. *He's going too fast.* Suddenly the trailer broke free and took on a new direction. In his rear view mirror the van driver saw his trailer hurtle into a line of parked cars.

At the other end of the street, two gardaí, who had witnessed the accident, turned and walked the other way. I guess they didn't fancy all that paperwork so close to logging off. I continued picking up gooey kitchen towels and found a £10 note by the kerb. My early morning helper and friend must have slept in at the YMCA.

I was ready to leave. With my hot dog stand in tow, I trundled towards Hawkins Street and sold the entire 90 newspapers to an ambitious newspaper salesman for £20. I then drove home, counted my money, and went to bed. I was more chuffed about the £20 for the newspapers than I was the other £700 made selling hot dogs.

The next day I put the sopping wet paper money into the oven to dry it out. The smell was sickening; legal tender and burnt pig did not mix well. They must have hated me in the bank.

* * *

These were the happiest days of my life because I was too busy to be any other way. I was making an ordinary man's fortune, I had plans to open a restaurant forming in my head, and life couldn't get better. I thought I had everything.

— CHAPTER FIVE —

The summer dragged on and the drug of success eventually wore off. I had been working my hot dog stand relentlessly for over two years and the money wasn't giving me a high anymore. Exhausted from the continuous graveyard shifts and lack of daylight, I was running on empty and suffering from pains in my chest. I needed a break, so I bought a Dawes Galaxy Tourer bike and decided to cycle around Europe.

Damien, my friend who gave me the initial idea of setting up the hotdog stand, took control of the business.

I had met him in town one day and he told me he needed a place to stay. I had just bought my first house and told him he could have a room in it. It all worked out nicely.

I left the chaos of Leeson Street for seven weeks and cycled over 2,000 miles around Europe. When I got back to Dublin I was fit as a fiddle and there was a drawer full of money inside my bedroom waiting to be counted. It was my cut from the hot dog trade. It sure felt good looking at all that money piled up for me. It came to over £5,000 and had materialised from thin air as far as I was concerned. Never in my life had I ever received such a gift of money.

* * *

Late November, having had my holiday, I began to work seven nights a week. There was simply too much money to be lost by taking a day off. It got busier and more hectic each night—35 Saturday nights in a row. I was making 50 kilos of fresh coleslaw every evening and what was left at the end of each session, if any, always went into one of the many empty mayonnaise buckets I had accumulated over the years.

Two nights of profit stick out in my mind. On 20 December, 1989 I grossed £800 and on 23 December, I sold 1,000 hot dogs. That morning I celebrated the beginning of my three day holiday by drinking half a bottle of port in bed and watching the Wizard of Oz until it became the Wozard of Wiz, and then I fell asleep.

Christmas Eve, Christmas Day and St Stephens' Day were the only three days in the year I remained closed, because Leeson Street was closed. God did not like drink to be sold on Christmas Day. I think it was okay to be in possession. One or two die-hard nightclubs did open at the end of Stephens' Day for the sad and lonely.

Christmas dinner with my mum and Eamon that year was cooked goose with *rot kraut und gloese* (like a spongy potato) which as a child I always called 'ohne kopf', 'without a head'.

That New Year's Eve was the busiest night of the year. Midnight was the eye of the storm, Sunday Bloody Sunday by U2 played loudly from one of the basements and then all hell broke loose.

10,000 people celebrating New Year's Eve on Leeson Street—it was like mating season in the jungle. I sold a hot dog, most of them with the works, every 14 seconds for a solid six hours. There were extended periods of time when a hot dog fired out of the hatch every three seconds. The queue remained 20 deep until 6.00 a.m. Trade continued until 7.30 a.m. I was a wreck.

When I got home it was 8.30 a.m. I emptied the black plastic bin liner full of paper money onto the floor and drank the second half of my bottle of port with the smell of used money wafting through the air.

I watched *Willy Wonka & the Chocolate Factory* on television, exhausted but content. I had sold a record 1,460 hot dogs.

* * *

Because I never re-used any of the leftover coleslaw, I now had 50 mayonnaise buckets filled with the stuff at varying stages of fermentation sitting in my back yard. One day I piled all the buckets into the back of my Peugeot and drove to the dump on Ballyogan Road. I enjoyed flinging each 10 kilo tub through the air and watching the contents explode on impact with the ground. The rats of the dump would soon hate the taste, sight and smell of rotten coleslaw.

January saw a downturn in hot dog sales, much as it had done the previous two years. People had no money after Christmas and it was freezing cold. Occasionally I'd see a girl walk the strip in a skimpy short skirt. She was no prostitute; this girl wasn't getting paid to be frozen stiff or stiffly unfrozen. A girl's capacity to endure the bitter cold in her attempt to find a loving mate can only be matched by her ability to then endure the pain of having his child.

During these quiet spells there was no need for the gas cooker to be on full power, in fact there wasn't even a need to have all three rings burning at the same time. The bones in my wrists cracked from the cold every time I picked up a ketchup bottle to line a frankfurter. I sometimes wondered why I even bothered to work on these bitter cold mornings, where I might sell as little as seventy hot dogs during a seven hour stint. But I was determined to provide a reliable service to my regulars, who sometimes travelled miles to buy a hot dog from my stand. Occasionally, on such a bitter cold night, I'd share a hot whisky with the garda on duty. We had one thing in common—neither of us wanted to be there on that freezing cold night. Those long cold nights—as bouncers sat inside warm nightclubs and I sat inside my hot dog stand serving the 'desperate for their hole' brigade—gave me character and earned me some respect. Not that the earned respect was much use to me later on, when it all began to fall apart.

* * *

It was the summer of 1990 and Ireland had reached the World Cup. Business was booming, so much so that I was no longer a one-man operation, but with the increase in sales came extra hassles, worries and complications. My employees worked four days a week and I slogged the longer, more work intensive weekends, beginning on a Thursday night, ending Sunday morning.

But there were problems. One Wednesday night, as I stood outside the hot dog stand preparing to go home, a customer asked me why I was now charging £1.50 for a hot dog.

'I'm not charging £1.50 for a hot dog.'

'Yes you are; I paid £1.50 for a hot dog at this stand last week.'

'You must have gone to one of the other hot dog stands,' I said.

'No, I was charged £1.50 at this hot dog stand.'

'Are you sure about that? I'm only charging £1.'

'Well that might be the case tonight, but I was definitely charged £1.50 last week.'

'I don't know how that's possible. I've never charged £1.50 for a hot dog.'

'It wasn't you that served me, but I was definitely charged £1.50.'

'And you're certain it was this stand?'

'Yes.'

'Okay, I'll look into it.'

I asked one of my helpers *Jack*, who was working that night, if he could shed any light on the matter. After a moment's hesitation he explained what was happening,

'Some of the lads wait until you've gone home and then they put the price of a hot dog up to £1.50. At the end of the night they count the bread that's left, work out your take and keep the difference.' Now I had vacancies.

I was grateful that *Jack* was a bit odd but honest.

Leeson Street was still a 'swim in the lake with a few hungry piranha' kind of a place, and calluses had formed on my psyche. I'd been trading for over three years, but felt in my gut that time was running out for my gold mine. Something would give; I didn't know what; maybe more competition would erode my turnover; maybe a garda made of tougher stuff would be drafted into the area.

I got on with the other three stall owners who had moved into the area following news of my business venture. They charged £1.50 for a hot dog, but I stood firm on £1. They were happy with more profit for less work; I preferred a higher turnover and a happier customer.

Apart from one time when I set up a picnic barbeque stand in front of my hot dog stand to sell burgers, we had no problems. Given the choice, customers preferred barbequed Quarter-Pounders to hot dogs.

'This better not be here next weekend or there's going to be trouble,' one of my rivals said, pointing at my barbeque stand.

There was more money to be made selling hot dogs than burgers, so threat and acumen blended into one and I went back to hot dogs.

Business continued to improve. In the early days; if a group of five people stood before me, one might have asked for a hot dog while the other four looked on in disgust. By the summer of 1990 it was four out of the five people who chose to eat a hot dog and at least two of them asked for seconds and thirds.

* * *

Ireland's success in the World Cup was directly reflected in my profits. That June, Ireland drew 1-1 with England. A late goal from Kevin Sheedy gave us one valuable point . . . and a reason to celebrate into the night.

When I arrived on Leeson Street, one of the students from the university *Jack* attended was waiting by my lamppost to tell me that he couldn't work that night because he was not feeling up to it.

Whenever someone didn't show up for work, I'd work that night myself. The way I saw it, I'd save the £40 wage and probably sell an extra 20 or 30 hot dogs. One of my tricks for improving sales on a quiet night was to keep customers standing near the hot dog stand as they ate. I'd make sure the hot dog was just perfect, to ensure a second sale. Any stragglers on the street would be drawn to the company of the hot dog stand. I think it was psychological; 'someone else is eating them, so they must be okay,' and I could chat to people until the cows came home, or the next customer came along. Eating my own hot dogs also inspired confidence.

'That's what I like to see—the chef eating his own food.'

Within half an hour the street was jammed with revellers. *Where the hell did all these people come from? And what were they doing out on a Monday night?*

I heard the alternative national anthem sung by boisterous boys and girls, 'Ole Ole Ole Ole,' repeated many times over. It became apparent to me that 1-1 against England in the World Cup was worth taking a sick day for; even if it was only the first match of the competition. I was swamped by a new crowd who were different from the regular late night revellers. These people were not looking for late night sleaze; most of them had rings on their fingers. These were elated football fans who had spilled into the night from an evening's celebration. I was sold out by midnight. *Fuck.*

There was no way I was losing out on 500 quid's worth of business.

I closed the hatch to disbelieving protests.

'I swear I've nothing left, BUT, I'LL BE BACK,' I promised and quickly drove home. I emptied the freezer of all bread rolls and frankfurters I had stored for emergencies. I grabbed six one-litre plastic bottles of ketchup and one litre of mustard and put everything into my car. On average, one litre of ketchup covered about 100 hot dogs; one litre of mild mustard covered about 500 hot dogs. I drove to all the late night Spar Shops in my vicinity and emptied dairy walls of frankfurters, even the turkey ones, and then I returned to Leeson Street.

The first hour was tricky because the bread rolls were still frozen. I turned up the flame under the frying pan and took my time with casual sauce-squirting and friendly chit chat, to give the bread time to thaw out and not lose anyone in the queue. By the second hour I was back up to speed, as everything had thawed out in the oven that was my workplace. I didn't have coleslaw, but people didn't seem to mind.

Dawn approached, the street emptied and I was up £650 thanks to Kevin Sheedy's goal. I reckoned that I had lost about 200 sales by not being prepared, but salvaged about 500 by being determined.

I was better prepared for the Holland match; also a 1-1 draw and I made another killing.

Houses were re-mortgaged and sick days used up by fans abroad. Later that June, Ireland was beaten 1-0 by Italy in the quarter finals. It was Saturday night and by now everyone had learnt the 'words' to 'Ole Ole Ole'.

Not ones to wallow in defeat, fans instead celebrated the fact that we were now ranked seventh in the world, and I celebrated because I was making a killing.

* * *

One night a German shepherd, almost certainly abandoned, appeared before me. He had hungry eyes, alert ears and a friendly tail. I threw him a split hot dog and he made it disappear so I threw him another one and he made that one disappear too. His tail continued to wag in anticipation. This game of 'swallow the hot dog' went on for ten more minutes and then he sat down on his honkers and watched me. People thought he was an innovative doorman. I stepped out of my hotdog stand to get something from the back of my hatchback. As the rear door went up the German shepherd jumped in and lay down. The autistic man in the mac who sometimes sat in my car to rest or sleep was happy of the company. I left them both and went back to work.

At 6.00a.m. I finished up and opened the rear door of my car. The German shepherd jumped out and ran around the car. My bleary-eyed friend stepped out and said he was going to go look for a bus. Before I had a chance to close the door, 'Rommel' had jumped back in again, happy with his new choice of owner.

* * *

Without a permanently valid licence, and vulnerable to the whims of individual gardaí, I knew that a fixed premises was the only way I could guarantee a continuation of this lucrative late night trade. I had my eye on a derelict basement located next to my hot dog pitch.

A tenant from an upper floor gave me the landlord's phone number. I wrote down everything I wanted to say about my proposal, so as not to stumble over any words, and then I made my phone call.

The telephone rang three times and a posh female voice answered. I introduced myself and after some swift formalities outlined my proposal to transform her dilapidated basement into a classy, middle-of-the-road restaurant/diner. She seemed to be suitably impressed by my telephone presentation.

The process of obtaining planning permission began shortly after I received the landlady's word that we had an agreement in principle. After three months free rent, I'd pay a non-refundable lump sum of six months rent—£5,000. This money was to be paid to the landlady, even if I didn't receive planning permission. I hired an architect to submit plans for a 24-seater restaurant, and when, four months later, the corporation declined me permission, I hired a consultant town planner to submit an appeal to An Bord Pleanála. All in all, applying for planning permission was an expensive procedure. I soon found myself doing battle with the view that my premises was going to be another restaurant with a wine licence, a music licence, and dance licence, ergo another nightclub in disguise. I argued strongly that it was a bona fide place of food.

My local TD, Ruairi Quinn, made representations on my behalf as a result of a meeting I had with him at his clinic. In the event of a successful application, I would take on a 35-year lease for the basement.

The months passed by.

As the decision date from An Bord Pleanala drew near the landlady demanded I pay the six months rent, which was now due.

She refused to sign a guarantee of my entitlement to a 35-year lease should planning permission be secured, though. The planning application was the applicant's prerogative, the permission, once granted, belonged to the building and its owner. If I were to be successful with my application I would be left vulnerable to a renegotiation of the 35-year lease, the value of which increased by my actions and investment. There was a stand-off and I threatened to withdraw my application altogether if the landlady did not give me that guarantee.

The basement's only inhabitant at this time, and I shuddered with revulsion when first I saw it, was an enormous grey rat, which lived in the prolific weed jungle growing tall from the basement floor. How the creature managed to climb the vertical stairs to peer at the world above was a mystery to me. But when human vibrations abated, I observed the sumo wrestling rat waddling along the pavement, until it disappeared into another basement. It was the size of a fat cat and fed itself on the thousands of half-eaten hotdogs, discarded over the railing into the rat's own Garden of Eden.

The days passed by. Nails were bitten to the quick. I spoke to the landlady's auctioneer—we all stood to lose money if I pulled out now. She'd get no rent and I'd lose money already invested. And each day I rang An Bord Pleanála for news.

* * *

One Tuesday morning I drove into the city to collect my hot dog stand. It was now parked on Hatch Street, around the corner from Leeson Street, because the gardaí had already towed it twice from the bus lane before the official 7 a.m. clearaway began. At £150-a-go it was an expensive oversleep. The lads didn't mind pulling the hot dog stand to safety when they finished their shift.

It was nearly seven in the morning and the rush hour traffic was getting organised. I lifted the cup of the tow-hitch onto the tow bar of my Peugeot and coughed an unpleasant cough. The back of my throat was dry and felt swollen. My forehead burned and my muscles ached. I was definitely coming down with something. Maybe stress had brought it on. I drove home. The unpleasant feeling at the back of my throat got worse. I couldn't swallow and my brain felt hot.

There were about 50 people ahead of me in St Vincent's Hospital's Accident and Emergency Department. The hours passed by irritatingly slowly and then a doctor told me I had a bad case of tonsillitis and that I should be admitted to the hospital. I was led to a ward, given a backless dressing gown and put into bed.

A nurse came by and slipped a thermometer into my mouth. She lifted her leg onto the bed to do something with her stocking. I didn't notice what it was she was doing with her stocking. She was blonde, slim, well endowed and in her early twenties. She had the most amazing legs—Marlene Dietrich division. I think she could see where my interests lay. I may have been ill but I was still able to appreciate the finer things. She looked at the thermometer and then asked me to turn over. Without warning she slipped something into my rectum.

'This is a suppository. It will help to reduce your temperature.'

On Thursday morning the doctor refused to discharge me, but I felt I had to get back to the Street, so I signed a form and discharged myself. They weren't happy about that in the hospital.

The next day the auctioneer phoned to inform me that the landlady had signed the contract guaranteeing my 35 year lease and on Monday morning I got my permission from An Bord Pleanala. Everything was coming together.

I wasn't feeling 100%, but I was excited about setting up my own diner. I saw it as a turning point in my life. It was, but in more ways than I might have wished.

* * *

Two weeks later, three of the four workmen I'd hired to build my restaurant walked into the empty rooms of the derelict basement. A six-panelled Georgian door was laid between a windowsill and a backless chair. One of the men opened a filthy sports bag, removed all tea-making paraphernalia and laid them on the new workman's breakfast table. We were ready to roll, but first came the inevitable banter, filled with stories of last night's drunken adventures, sexual exploits and social disasters.

The men ranged in age and size. The eldest had bushy grey hair and a face ragged from social alcohol abuse. Pink pouches hung like deflated bagpipes under his red eyes and an infestation of wrinkles ran rampant about his face like a Spirograph drawing.

The kettle boiled, dust rose and four mugs were filled. Tea bags inflated like airbags.

'Do you take milk?' he asked me.

'Loads please and one sugar.'

I wore a brand new navy boiler suit and had a white dust mask resting on my head, which looked like a swollen skullcap. I was eager to get started with the job and do whatever I could to help. The rented basement was doing to my funds what dry rot had been doing to the wooden floorboards for decades.

'Ah no, take out my tea bag first,' the youngest workman exclaimed. He had short blonde hair, smooth boyish skin and was teenage slim.

A tea bag was fished out of a mug using a long nail. Steaming and dripping, the bag fell to the wooden floor with a thud. The slurps, the chewing, and the nose whistling continued unabated. A blind man would have sworn a dozen people were feeding at the same time.

Soon, the fourth workman arrived. He was in his mid-twenties, had short black curly hair and a small button nose. A lifetime of smiles baked onto his face gave him the appearance of a friendly garden gnome. His bloodshot eyes and yellow teeth were the result of a nicotine and alcohol addiction. The pupils in the whites of his eyes looked like dead flies caught in a red web.

After more conversation about the price of prostitutes and errant contraceptive devices, we were finally ready to get to work. I was eager. I put on my brand new work gloves, pulled down my virgin dust mask, adjusted my scratch free protective face goggles and put on my shiny red builders hat. Within minutes the five of us got to work with our sledgehammers and shovels. Day became night as the old ceiling made of laths and plaster came crumbling down.

For a moment the hanging ceiling looked like the broken wing of a huge prehistoric bird before it buckled and collapsed onto the floor. This was the birth of The Hungry Wolf.

* * *

Well it seems to me that everyone has a Bono story to tell or sell these days, and I'm no different.

While working on my basement premises during the day, I was still a familiar figure almost every night of the week at the hot dog stand. A long black limo with tinted windows pulled up one night and the driver got out. He ordered six of the best and asked me to make them gourmet, for 'the boys', who apparently were fans.

A week later, I got a phone call from Principle Management and was asked to provide hot dogs for a small gathering. U2 and friends had hired the Savoy Cinema for a private showing of Terminator 2.

I arrived at the Savoy with my newest girlfriend around 7.30 p.m. The security men could see that we were the hot dog providers for the evening by the cooker, bottle of gas, frankfurters and bread rolls we held under our arms. We set up on a table provided and were asked to join the others in the auditorium. As soon as the nasty metal thing from the future was vaporised in the cauldron, I returned to the foyer to begin hot dog production. Five minutes later the guests began to fill the foyer and I became the pied piper of the perfect waistline.

The girls were as hungry as the men yet there wasn't a single fat one in the harem. The clothes and the make up made all these people look like a delegation from another Galaxy. When it was all over and the long black limos had filled to capacity, Bono came over to me, shook my hand, and thanked me for coming.

— CHAPTER SIX —

One evening, just as I set off for work, I saw in my rear view mirror that the hot dog stand had somehow severed itself from the back of my car and was now veering towards a parked BMW. It took me about half a second to do the calculations and then I hit the brakes. The ensuing collision with the out-of-control hot dog stand caused a nasty dent in the back of my car, but hitting the BMW would have put a nasty dent in my wallet. It could have been worse, but I shrugged it off as an accident.

The restaurant venture was causing all manner of headaches. The company I bought my kitchen equipment from went bust a week after I put down a £1,500 deposit. I got a phone call from the salesman who had sold me the equipment to say that my money was gone but I should try doing a deal with the Receiver who was in Dundalk with my equipment.

'Tell me the bit about my money being lost?' I asked.

God was I pissed off with that salesman—he must have known that there was a serious problem with the company, yet he took my money and shook my hand knowing there was a good chance I'd never see the equipment or get my deposit back. The salesman gave me the exact location of the warehouse in Dundalk. I had to get to my equipment before the Receiver flogged it to the first person who came along with hard cash.

Lucky for me, my friend Jens had a big white van and we drove to Dundalk that same day and found the warehouse which was housing my equipment. The Receiver was a horrible man.

'Anybody who's stupid enough to pay a deposit deserves to lose their money,' he said.

What on earth do you say to someone like that?

I paid in cash—no other form of payment was acceptable—and we loaded up the van and drove back to Dublin. I stored the equipment in my home until the restaurant was ready for it.

Building the restaurant, which was designed by Jens, took up most of 1991, with the hot dog stand funding the entire project. A supporting wall was removed in the basement to make better use of the two rooms and decent sized toilets were installed on the left hand side. Staff toilets were put in at the far back left of the restaurant together with a network of plumbing and water storage. The entire restaurant was newly wired. A top of the range stainless-steel kitchen was fitted on the right hand side of the premises. The kitchen had a four-ring gas cooker and a pizza oven that needed a minimum of six people to manoeuvre and was built into the chimney breast. It had a long fridge with a stainless-steel counter, a dough mixer and plenty of stainless-steel shelving. At the very back of the restaurant there were more sinks and chopping surfaces—these were the kitchen porter's quarters. There was a large serving hatch which separated the kitchen from the dining area and an undulating ash counter which snaked to one side of the restaurant, and then the line of the counter continued on as a wooden bench inlaid with dark green cushion. The bench ran along two walls of the restaurant to the front entrance. The floor was made of Mexican terracotta tiles which were waxed and buffed. The tables had wrought iron bases with pine tops. I had official seating for 24 persons, but could inflate it to around 50 punters, if I had to. During the evening, down lighters would be dimmed to create a romantic atmosphere and compliment the candles on the dining tables.

Apart from the removal of the internal wall, which had been carried out by a team of highly paid, highly insured professionals, the remaining workforce were tea-break labourers. Completion dates were made and broken. We all worked hard, including friends. With all the pressures of setting up in business, myself and my girlfriend grew apart and soon I was single again.

My German shepherd Rommel disappeared too. I took him to the shops one day, and as usual he sat obediently by the entrance. I turned around to pay for my groceries, and when I looked back, he was gone. It was a shame. I liked that dog, and his presence in my home might have changed the events that later took place.

* * *

A couple of weeks before Christmas 1991, The Hungry Wolf opened its doors. Now I had two businesses making money on Leeson Street and it felt good. On New Year's Eve, my recently departed girlfriend and another ex-girlfriend came to dine in my restaurant with their families, which was a nice sign of support.

By the spring of 1992 I was on top of the world. The Hungry Wolf stayed open 18 hours a day. The evening menu began at 6 p.m. and by midnight it had blended into the late night session, which stormed ahead until 7 a.m. At 11.30 a.m. the lunch staff arrived to begin their preparations.

I was faced with a whole set of problems that were new to me though. Hanging on to good staff wasn't always easy. One night a bouncer from a nightclub, enjoying a hearty breakfast, spotted a talented girl whizzing around the floor doing six things at the same time and offered her more money to work in his nightclub. Bouncers always referred to the nightclubs they worked in as their own.

There was no such a thing as one month's notice or even one week's notice—the girl simply didn't turn up for work. For the nightclubs, offering more money was easy, because they had a lot more cash behind them, charging what they did. I was a simple restaurant charging reasonable prices. I explained this to the poaching bouncer. He accepted my argument and the defections ended.

But there were other problems.

At The Hungry Wolf, dishes were breaking at a horrendous rate. One night, as I walked into the kitchen, I saw a kitchen porter slap a plate down onto the steel rim of the waste food bin. He was too lazy to scrape the leftover food with a knife. The plate cracked and without so much as a flinch, he dropped the two halves into the bin and picked up the next plate.

'Please don't do that again,' I said.

'Sure, okay,' he replied, as if it didn't matter to him either way.

£500 worth of dishes had been lost in the first month, most of it late at night. I didn't know what to do, apart from asking the staff to be more careful. I felt that if I charged the staff for all the breakages, they would steal the difference some other way and there was no way of proving who was responsible for each individual breakage. Penalising responsible staff was something I didn't want to do. Eventually I bought unbreakable plates for the late night trade, but they looked ugly and felt like flattened tin.

One of my waitresses put a foil-wrapped potato into the commercial microwave to bake it, and instead nearly re-created the London Blitz. She was a good, honest waitress, but she had her moments. One day as I emptied the coins out of the pay phone, she asked me, 'Does the money customers put in not pay the bill automatically?' I thought it was cute, and tried not to laugh when I explained that the money in the phone box couldn't travel down the phone line and had to actually be brought to the phone company.

Selling hot dogs was so much simpler, but even that was starting to cause more problems.

The Health Inspector walked into the restaurant to do a routine inspection one day. The examination went well because the kitchen was built to a high standard and was spotlessly clean. On his way out he turned to me and said, 'Oh yes, I almost forgot, this is for you.'

I looked at the bundle of papers he thrust into my hand. It was a summons for an untidy hot dog stand. I thought it was sneaky—he used an official visit to inspect the restaurant to serve me with a summons for the hot dog stand.

I was starting to learn that in business, there are a lot of sneaky people and you always had to keep your wits about you. But business people at least operated, more or less, within the law.

* * *

Then it all started to go wrong. One evening I arrived on Leeson Street to find a hot dog stand, which looked remarkably like my own hot dog stand, parked in front of my restaurant. This unwelcome stranger was clearly breaking the street trading code. There was a more accommodating place to position a new food stall in between two already established ones— like somewhere in the middle. This would have left the newcomer outside the entrances of three busy nightclubs. A move like that would have required brass balls—the nightclubs wouldn't have wanted the new food stall directly outside their premises—but business would have boomed for the newcomer. However, the intruder chose my spot. My hard earned trading pitch: established over years of working freezing cold nights, when no other food stalls bothered to turn up. Dead nights, when my bones cracked with the cold and my eye lids weighed heavily on my eyeballs . . .

I double parked my car and approached the wooden hut. I was instantly taken aback. I recognised the man. He had been lurking around Leeson Street for a while, staring me out.

'Hi, you're a little close aren't you?' I said, trying to regain my composure.

'What do you mean?' he asked. I didn't believe he didn't know what I was talking about.

'You're on my pitch. Could you not at least move up the road a little?'

After five years of street trading I knew not to antagonise a wrong doer.

'It's not up to me; you'll have to talk to the boss.'

'And where would he or she be?'

'He'll be back in a couple of hours.'

I looked at the man and tried to read behind his opaque eyes. There was something about this guy I didn't like. He had a smug look upon his face, yet he pretended to be helpless at the same time. He was hiding something behind that cocky smile.

'Fair enough,' I said and returned to crank up my own hot dog stand. Something was up. Something was definitely up.

— CHAPTER SEVEN —

My two hot dog sellers were late that night. I squeezed the hitch-lever and lifted the hot dog stand from the tow bar of my car. There were cars parked all along my side of the street. I had to push the hot dog stand 25 feet down the road before I found a gap. It was a tight squeeze in between two parked cars. There were never this many cars parked here at 10.30p.m.

I suspected that one or two of the strategically parked cars may have belonged to the new competition. I unlocked the back door, stepped over supplies and lit the gas lamp. A dim light came on with a hiss. The delicate mantel was torn at the base and needed changing. I opened the serving hatch to let in some light. The edge of the hatch barely made it past the back of the brand new Land Rover. The last thing I needed right now was hassle with the owner of this expensive vehicle. The carcass of the metal gas lamp was stubborn to come apart and the filament mantel broke off. It fell to the floor and vaporised into fine dust. I tied the new mantel net around the gas feed nozzle, put the lamp back together again and lit the bottom of the mantel. For a moment it hung like a used condom.

What an awful smell; the body of ash spread upwards like a forest fire. While the new filament mantel formed I poured water into the pot and lit the gas cooker.

Then one of the other hot dog stand vendors approached me.

'Wolfie, this is not good. The Garda aren't going to tolerate it,' he said, pointing at the new stall.

'Your man says his boss will be around in a couple of hour's time,' I replied.

'You have to talk to him. You talk better than us.'

'I'll see what I can do. I don't understand why he's opened up on my pitch,' I said.

'He'll get us all shut all down, there are enough of us here already.'

'I'll see what this new guy is like; maybe I can talk him into moving up the road a little.'

'You'll need to do more than that. He can't stay.'

'There's something unusual about him, he's not nervous or worried at all, considering he's opened up on someone else's pitch,' I said.

'You're alright; you've got your restaurant to fall back on,' grumbled the hot dog seller and walked back towards his own food stall. It was true—I did have my own restaurant, but I didn't want to lose my lucrative hot dog stand just yet.

I was confused by the trader's manner. He was a hard man—why ask me to convince someone away from the street, so fervently, even if I did speak better English than he did?

I turned on the gas and lit the mantel. It blew up bright like a supernova. The inside of the hot dog stand was a mess. Dried in ketchup and mustard stains and streaks of oily coleslaw were still smeared on both shelves. The floor was filthy with thickened smudges of mud and black scuff marks. No wonder I was in trouble with the Health Inspector.

With the restaurant becoming busier and eating up all of my time there was little of it left for the hot dog stand anymore. The lads did everything—well they were meant to do everything—they were getting well paid for it; £50 cash each, per night.

Still the little wagon was a good earner and financial back-up for the expense-hungry restaurant, with its high wage bills, rent, rates, insurance, leased equipment and other miscellaneous costs.

* * *

At that time, the late night trade in The Hungry Wolf was flourishing. The place was one of the first classy diners to serve food all night long in the pre-boom city of Dublin and I was already making plans for The Hungry Wolf 2.

But the arrival of this new hot dog stand had an ominous feel about it. The boldness of opening up on my pitch, outside my restaurant, using my colours, was more than coincidental. This was planned and there was a reason why I was the one targeted. Maybe the owner saw my lucrative pitch as the point of least resistance on Leeson Street, because I was only one person.

I was getting tired of working these Vampire hours, the late afternoon breakfasts, the lack of sunlight and restricted social life that wasn't meant to come until I had kids. I wanted a normal lifestyle, with normal trading hours. I wanted the evening experience to flourish.

I walked down the diagonal metal stairs and went into my restaurant.

Just two tables were occupied.

Unlike the late trade, the evening trade was not flourishing as I hoped it would, even though the food was mouth watering and reasonably priced.

Leeson Street had a reputation for expensive plonk, a last chance to get laid, and vomit; not the kind of place to take your partner for a romantic evening meal.

In The Hungry Wolf, £10 bought a starter and a main course. A bottle of house wine was £7. 'Rip off Ireland' did not exist in my establishment.

Local hotel doormen forwarded me some guests, for which they received a commission. When asked by a tourist, 'Where's a good place to eat?' the doorman could respond by recommending several establishments. But there were a lot of restaurants offering bribes to doormen and I imagine many of them could pad the brown envelope better than I.

Some evenings my restaurant was full; however some evenings the takings weren't enough to pay constant wage bills and other associated costs.

But I persisted and concentrated on offering value for money in the same way my hot dog stand did. I believed in treating the customer fairly. If they were treated well, they would come back, or stay all night. I remember a couple from Belfast. They arrived one evening looking for a romantic dinner. He was in high spirits—perhaps it was the something 'banned' he inhaled from his asthma device—so he told me. And I think she was happy for him, as girls so often are. I loved the accent—don't mess with me, words rolling over one another with a rising intonation.

The guitarist twanged away quietly in the candlelit background and the waitresses looked fabulous in their leggings and skin tight vests. As midnight approached and the restaurant emptied of its four other clients, the gentleman from the North ordered another two Irish coffees in the hope of prolonging the evening. By the time the final blob of fresh cream had settled, the restaurant began to fill with late night punters and the couple's evening continued until long after they ordered breakfast at 4.30 a.m.

I had soon realised that the real money was made after-hours, when nightclubs reigned and wallets lost their inhibitions.

The only drawback was that there was a variety of typical staff problems and the best way to keep an eye on things was for me to be on the premises all the time. This was why I wanted the evening trade to be profitable, because five years of working these unsociable hours had drained me. I felt I had worked my means to an end.

* * *

My two hot dog sellers eventually arrived. They'd had a few beers in the pub. It was lucky for me the pubs closed at 11.30 p.m. or there may have been nights when I never got to see my hot dog sellers at all. I knew the consumption of alcohol would slow them down, but I didn't mind too much. That's why I had two of them doing my old job.

I'd once worked a night under the influence of four beers. Next day I counted 200 fewer hot dogs sold— that never happened to me again. But I couldn't deny my hot dog sellers a few to get them through the long, stifling night. They were, after all, students on a wage, working a weekend night—a sacrifice if ever there was one.

Re-designed, the inside of the hot dog stand was now a marvel of ergonomics and the two students had been able to maintain a constant supply of hot dogs to a queuing public. They each had their own bucket of coleslaw, a plastic tongs, stack of kitchen towels, ketchup and mustard bottles and boxes of bread rolls. They took turns replenishing the frankfurter pots and their turnover equalled that of my own when charged up for a hectic session.

I looked at my watch. It was 11.15p.m. I had to get back home for a quick bath and a change of clothes. I was taking a couple of hours off work and going to a party with my new girlfriend.

I had met her during one of my late morning leaflet drops to surrounding businesses. This proved an ideal way of drumming up business for the lunch trade—secretaries and other employees were an hour or so away from their lunch breaks; stomachs growled as a reasonably priced, mouth watering menu was placed teasingly before their eyes. This exercise in entrepreneurialism was also a door opener to acquainting many girls stationed behind office furniture. My new girlfriend had hundreds of friends, and was always going to parties, and I was happy to tag along.

I returned to Leeson Street at midnight and double parked alongside my hot dog stand. Customers were queued in twos, jammed in between my counter and the back of the Land Rover. The Land Rover already had splotches of coleslaw clinging to it. Soon people would be sitting on the bonnet as late night rules on street etiquette kicked in. With a bit of luck the owner of the brand new vehicle would return from a healthy night of drinking, too hammered to notice or care.

It was always a nerve racking experience when a car parked in front of my hot dog stand began to reverse whilst indicating right to join the flow of traffic.

A quick vault over the counter and a hard slap on the boot of the moving vehicle usually sent the right message to the reaction impaired driver.

It was then that I noticed a group of men standing on the granite steps of a nearby building. Three of them I recognised: they were the hot dog sellers who ran the other hot dog stands on Leeson Street. The fourth man I'd never seen before. He was a large, heavy man with a bloated ruddy face that exuded evil and hate. Standing on the top granite step he towered above them all.

I assumed they were talking about the new vendor in our patch, so I reluctantly approached to lend my support as promised.

'WHO THE FUCK ARE YOU?' the vicious voice snarled as I stood on the periphery of the group. The words were spoken with a hardened Dublin city dialect and pinned to me with a threatening finger. I was a little stunned. I hadn't said a word and already this man had condemned me. I could have been someone looking for directions to a night club or a taxi rank.

'Well . . . I own that hot dog stand,' I answered hesitantly and turned my head to identify which one. When I looked back the human boar was glaring at me, his bitter eyes eating into my very existence. Even from a few feet away, I could smell the man, and it wasn't pleasant. There was nothing pleasant about him.

'YOU'RE ONLY A FUCKING GERMAN,' he said slowly.

'IF I EVER FUCKING SEE YOU LOOK IN MY FUCKING DIRECTION AGAIN; YOUR FUCKING HOT DOG STAND, YOUR FUCKING

RESTAURANT AND YOUR FUCKING HOME,
WILL BE BURNT TO THE FUCKING GROUND.
NOW FUCK OFF.'

My heartbeat crunched up a gear as I walked back
towards The Hungry Wolf. I didn't turn around to get
a second opinion. In fact it was all I could do not to
miss the entrance of my restaurant altogether.

My girlfriend was sitting on a high chair at the
counter waiting for me. I joined her for a glass of
house red. My eyes wandered around the room, and
I concentrated on looking at the decorated plates that
hung high on the walls, while I regained my composure.
Finally my gaze landed on the tip bowl by the cash
register; '*Pour la fumé*' was written on a piece of paper
and sellotaped around its side.

'Is everything okay?' she asked.

'Can we stay down here a little while—maybe have
a bite to eat before we go out?'

'Sure, okay,' she said and smiled.

The bulldog-faced man from the granite steps
obviously knew more about me than he'd first implied.
He ran the new hot dog stand. But that was my pitch
up there—it represented five years of hard graft. I'd
stand my ground, arrive on Leeson Street earlier
tomorrow evening and set up my hot dog stand outside
my restaurant.

About half an hour later I climbed the stairs to see
the lay of the land. The boar was gone but his copycat
hot dog stand was still parked on Leeson Street, but
it was now closed. One of the traders was standing

outside his own hot dog stand. As soon as he saw me, he walked over.

'Who on earth was that?' I asked. 'I'm not going near him again.'

'That's The General,' he replied, and I began to worry.

The following night I arrived two hours early to claim my pitch. I was the first one to arrive.

— CHAPTER EIGHT —

I had met The General, or Martin Cahill, as the priest baptised him. He was the kind of man who would harm an innocent person to send a message to an innocent victim. He began his criminal career as a house burglar and morphed into a dangerous gangster with a cancerous attitude problem. He was an anti-Christ who needed the threat of violence and hurt to gain a respect he never received. Cahill was nothing more than a rash on the city—an incurable rash. Though I didn't know all of these facts at the time, I knew he was a bad person. I just didn't recognise him. Maybe I would have if he had spoken to me with his hand pressed up against his face, like he appeared in newspaper photos and on TV.

I had heard of Cahill. I knew he had pulled off the most famous robbery in the history of the Irish State when he stole 17 artworks worth over £30 million from the Beit Collection at Russborough House, County Wicklow.

While I was running around Dublin searching for a cheap cooker and a way to start my business, he was

Right: Luckily, I had the know-how and the tools to build the hot dog stand myself. Starting off with the frame of a horse box and a few boards of plywood, I put my new 'business premises' together in my friend's back garden.
© *Author's private collection*

Below: Maybe the reason for my poor sales early on was the look of my brown, wooden box. Things would improve, I told myself, once I got it painted.
© *Author's private collection*

Business boomed as my hot dog stand became the focus of attention for late-night revellers spilling out of the nightclubs, looking for decent food at a decent price. © *Author's private collection*

Above: Martin Cahill, the notorious criminal known as 'The General' was the bane of my life. Few people got to see what he looked like. I was unfortunate enough to be one of them. © *Photocall Ireland*

Right: The Hungry Wolf was open 18 hours a day. It brought new challenges and new problems, but trade flourished for a time. © *Author's private collection*

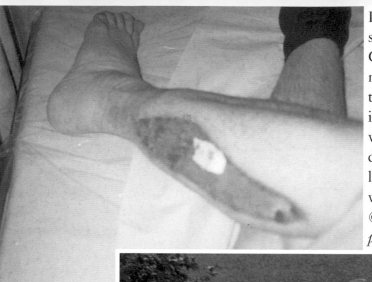

Left: I was shot by The General's men in a way that would inflict the worst possible damage to my leg. The wound was horrific.
© *Author's private collection*

Right: I was busy painting my house when I heard the news that The General had been killed. My disbelief turned to relief and delight when I realised my ordeal was over. In spite of everything that happened, I still felt sorry for Cahill. Nobody deserves to die the way he did.
© *Photocall Ireland*

conducting his own search for suitable buyers for the stolen paintings.

He was a brutal figure. He had burgled the offices of the Director of Public Prosecutions and stole more than 150 files relating not only to him but to other high profile cases.

I had seen his story on RTÉ's *Today Tonight* programme which revealed him to be the suspected mastermind behind numerous high-profile crimes dating back to 1974. He was reputedly worth several million pounds. Despite having three cars, including a Mercedes, and a luxury house worth almost £1 million, he still claimed the dole. This fact, more than anything else, had seemed to anger the Government and questions were asked in the Dáil.

An investigation resulted in his welfare payments being stopped, prompting some newspapers to run the headline, 'Unemployment Down by One'. But soon after, he had appeared in court on charges of threatening his neighbours. After an all-day hearing the case was adjourned for a week. Following the hearing, Cahill was arrested for a breach of the peace. On emerging from the court in his balaclava, he started to sing and took off his clothes to reveal a Mickey Mouse decorated t-shirt and boxer-shorts. He was arrested and taken into the Bridewell Garda Station.

He seemed a colourful character, but I didn't take much notice. Why would I? He had nothing to do with me. Even the fact that we were now neighbours didn't bother me. After all, why would a rich gangster be interested in a lowly hot dog vendor like me?

But The General's moment in the spotlight had proved to be disastrous for his career. Embarrassed into action, the Garda had assigned more than 90 officers to his case, involving 24-hour surveillance that more or less eliminated his chances of organising any sort of big-time crimes.

Many of his lieutenants had cracked under the pressure and retreated into the shadows or were arrested for a range of offences, but Cahill took it as a personal slight and infuriated the Garda with persistent mockery and intimidation.

Some said he was losing control, but this meant he was at his most dangerous. Unable to pull off any large heists under such scrutiny, Cahill started to look to other ways of making money.

Having frequented a club on Leeson Street, his eyes started to turn to the profitable businesses along it. And that's where I came into the picture. Cahill wanted to enter the hot dog business.

* * *

The restaurant was beginning to fill up; it was going to be another busy night. My girlfriend and I went to the party. We sat around drinking and a girl started singing. She had a soulful voice. This was a real down to earth party. The task of singing changed hands like a baton at a relay race. For a while, I forgot my troubles.

At four in the morning we left the party. Still, even on my days off, like a mother checking in on her child after a night out, I liked to check in on both my shops. When we arrived, Leeson Street looked deserted. I expected to see tumbleweed rolling down the street. My hot dog stand, by now a permanent fixture on late night Leeson Street, was gone. All the hot dog stands were gone. I went into the restaurant to find out what had happened but nobody could give me an answer. The girls were too busy serving a multitude of hungry people. Everybody was so busy that they didn't even have time to clean the toilets.

A drunken, fat woman had vomited all over the toilets, as well as leaving various excretements behind. The Ladies was in a very bad way, covered with unspeakable filth, and needed immediate attention. There was nothing else for it. Holding back the urge to gag on the rancid fumes, I closed the toilets temporarily and got to work, removing blockages and cleaning up all sorts of disgusting debris. Nobody would mind if the women used the Gents for a while, but I was soon able to re-open the Ladies, hoping I'd never have to repeat the cleaning job I'd just undertaken.

Eventually I found one of my hot dog sellers. He was chatting up a girl at the back of the restaurant, sitting on the steps, leaning against the wall under the moonlight. They were sharing a bottle of house red. He told me the Garda had taken the hot dog stand and that there was nothing he could have done to prevent it. My hot dog stand was now sitting in Harcourt

Terrace Garda Station. He told me that when the police arrived all the other stall owners packed up and left. Mine was the only one that didn't have an owner there to protect it.

I wasn't sure what to do. Drive to Harcourt Terrace Garda Station? With alcohol consumed? What could I possibly achieve by going there now?

The disgusting fat woman with blood on her hands was falling about the restaurant shouting profanities—she looked like she might even get sick again. Using the skills of a sheep dog I herded her out of the restaurant. She hadn't paid for her food or wine—it wasn't worth pursuing. I thought to myself that I really needed a doorman.

Oblivious to all of life's problems and my problems, the 50 or so patrons drank wine from tea pots, ate pizzas, pastas and steak sandwiches. They talked and they laughed and The Rolling Stones' *Sympathy for the Devil* warned of things to come.

Then the menu changed to breakfasts only. You just can't beat a bacon/sausage and fried egg sandwich with a cup of fresh tea at 4.30 a.m. with your head still spinning from a night not yet over. One large man, a TV presenter, ate seven full Irish breakfasts, one after another, and said it was the best £35 he'd ever spent.

Two coffees later, curiosity got the better of me and I climbed the diagonal staircase to my car. My girlfriend was getting tired and wanted to go home. With the nightclubs shut and no hot dog stands present to provide a valid reason for hanging around, there was no one left on Leeson Street. Apart from a few taxis—the dark days of the monopoly—there was no other traffic on the roads.

As I arrived at Harcourt Terrace Garda Station—the car pound was located behind it—I slowed down and stopped. *That's odd*, I thought.

A garda appeared from behind a wall, our eyes met, and then he disappeared into the back of the station. He seemed to be in a hurry and he had looked at me with some suspicion. I decided to go home, get some sleep and come back later on that day, because my second wind had come and gone and I suddenly felt shattered.

It was daylight when we arrived outside my house on Belmont Avenue and the birds were already chattering their morning gossip. We went straight to bed.

Four hours later the phone rang and yanked me out of a dream.

I picked up the telephone.

'Hello.'

'Mr Eulitz, I'm calling from Harcourt Terrace Garda Station. Would you mind calling down to the station as soon as possible?'

'Okay, I'll be there in 20 minutes,' I yawned, still half asleep, and scratched the back of my head. This would be a simple enough matter of collecting the hot dog stand and finding out why it was towed, during late night trading hours, after five years of not being towed. I made myself a cup of tea to boot up my brain. My girlfriend stayed in bed.

'I'll be back in an hour or so,' I said.

'Okay,' she said and turned over. I made a second cup of tea and took it with me into the car. I was proficient at driving my car whilst drinking a cup of tea, if necessary using both my knees to steer.

When I arrived at the Garda Station I was beckoned into a small concrete room. The room had a scratched old table, two chairs and was badly in need of a paint job. How alleged criminals had found the time to scratch their initials onto the wooden table was a mystery to me—maybe they did it during the good cop bad cop changeover. We sat down and were quickly joined by three more gardaí. The room suddenly looked full.

'This is a bit over the top for an impounded hot dog stand,' I said.

'Could you tell us your exact whereabouts this morning between 4.00 a.m. and 5.00 a.m.?' one garda asked me.

'You want to know where I was this morning?'

'Yes, between 4 a.m. and 5 a.m.'

After a few moments of trying to assimilate what was going on I explained my whereabouts right up to the point of seeing the garda dart into the back of the Garda Station. They all seemed to take turns looking at each other and then one of them asked me, 'What were you doing outside the Garda Station at 5 a.m.? Why didn't you call in? Why did you drive away when the garda saw you?'

'I didn't drive away because he saw me, I decided to go home and pick up the hot dog stand later.'

I repeated my whereabouts a second time, emphasising that I was very tired, leaving out the few drinks I'd had, and that I just wanted to go home to my bed.

'Okay.'

'Why do you ask?'

'And your girlfriend, can she confirm this?'

'Yes, together with about thirty people from the party, not to mention the staff in my restaurant, why, what's wrong?'

Eventually the garda told me that my hot dog stand had been set alight at approximately 4.50 a.m. in the car pound at the back of the Garda Station.

'What! You're joking?'

'No, you'd better come and take a look for yourself.'

As it turned out, the garda I'd seen at 5 a.m. was running to get a bucket of water to throw on the fire when he saw me pull up in my car. *They still put out fires with buckets of water?*

I could see how it seemed a strange coincidence that I happened to be outside the Garda Station at the time of the fire and not call in. But what was my motive? The hot dog stand wasn't even insured; I didn't think you could insure such a business.

'I don't suppose you have security cameras?' I asked.

'I'm afraid not.'

Video footage or not, common sense told us who the guilty thug was. And then it became clear to me what had happened.

When the Garda realised that it was the infamous General who was the muscle behind the latest food stall to arrive on Leeson Street, they decided to shut him down immediately. They were not going to allow that thug take root on Leeson Street, and the only sure way of closing him down, without a valid counter argument, was to get rid of the original hot dog stand, the one that had previously shown some clout. They had impounded Cahill's hot dog stand to his disbelief. In frustration, he burned down my stand.

* * *

The inside of the hot dog stand was charred badly and smelled like a giant ashtray filled with cigarette butts and spilled Guinness. Paint had melted and run tears down the wall. Some had peeled into a brittle tongue. Memories tumbled back. The months I'd spent building the hot dog stand at the back of Jens's parents' property and the years I spent perfecting its internal design, working in it, living it, being its central nervous system. A piece of me was in that hot dog stand and now that piece was burnt out. How could someone do such a horrible thing and for what purpose?

I soon found out. The General believed that I had made a deal with the Garda to clear Leeson Street of all food stalls for the benefit of my restaurant. Nothing could have been further from the truth. The hot dog stand had always been more net-profitable than the restaurant. And only somebody in the food business would have known that the hot dog eating customer and the more discerning restaurant clientele were two separate markets.

There was very little overlap. One customer wanted a hot dog, a quick junk fix, and the other wanted a breakfast, a steak sandwich, a pizza, a pasta dish or a cup of tea . . . and the restaurant could never fit more than 50 people, no matter how many queued to get in.

The General didn't even deny that he had torched my hot dog stand. When I met one of his cronies later, he whispered in my ear that they knew my mother drove a silver Honda Civic.

When The General burnt out my hot dog stand as it stood impounded in the Garda station, he had, in his evil way, struck two birds with one stone. The General had an unnatural hatred of the Garda; I imagine even the ones I suspected he was dealing with.

This was the beginning of what quickly turned into a prolonged nightmare.

* * *

There followed a 'cold war' type stand off between Martin Cahill and the Garda. Every weekend, his wooden hut would arrive on Leeson Street and he parked on my old trading patch. The evil thug then sat himself down on the wide granite footsteps of the adjacent building and watched with the patience of a serial killer. He didn't trade or even attempt to trade, for to do so would have led to an immediate arrest. A game was being played out.

Every weekend the hut arrived and this psychotic thug sat by its side, like a street dog marking his territory. Thinking about stolen paintings, I imagine.

An older garda from Harcourt Terrace Station informed me that I wouldn't be able to claim compensation for my burnt out hot dog stand, because at the time of the incident the hot dog stand was impounded and technically belonged to them. I hadn't enquired about claiming compensation from the Garda and his suggestion irritated me.

'So you're telling me that you can tow away any vehicle and not be responsible for it at all?' The garda looked at me with his 'I never got promoted' face and twisted it into a false smile. Talk about infuriating the victim. I had no intention of claiming anything; it wasn't the Garda who had burnt out my hot dog stand, although pathetically enough they let it happen right under their noses.

I refused to be beaten. I had another idea. I'd always felt that one day my street trading enterprise might come to a sudden end, though not at the hands of a vicious malefactor. I was fighting a two-front war, with The General on one side and the Garda on the other.

* * *

I remembered calling into the Civic Offices in 1987 to speak with someone about making my business fully legitimate. There had to be some kind of proper licence I could buy—something more substantial than my ineffective £175 Trading Licence—to sell hot dogs in a public area, especially one as hungry as late night Leeson Street. Not knowing every week whether I had a job or not was stressful on top of exhausting.

It was during my conversation with the woman behind the thickened glass window that she told me the police had no jurisdiction over food trading on private property. That was interesting, I thought. Of course the tricky bit was finding a privately owned site in just the right part of the city and getting the owner of this lucrative spot to give his or her permission for me to trade on it. I hoped that I would never need to do this. Hope, however, is a blind man not stepping in dog shit.

* * *

I called into the metal merchants who had made the diagonal staircase and all the stainless-steel shelving in the kitchen. I asked them to make me a two metre wide platform, which would sit on brackets screwed into the wall of the main building above my restaurant and rest on the concrete support block of the footpath railing—allowing ample headroom for customers descending the stairs into my restaurant. I designed a bullet shaped, stainless-steel hot dog stand and had it made by the same metal fabricators. It was a two cubic meter treasure trove containing a gas-powered fridge, a water boiler with two sinks and a powerful single ring gas cooker. Half litre sized steel compartments embraced the outer lower half of the large pot to allow for bread toasting and a perforated metal sheet divided the pot into two equal sections. An arched roof was fixed four feet above the counter. It had a square lip on either side to divert rainwater in case of scattered showers. A bright gas lamp hung underneath the roof, which reflected heat and illuminated the space age hot dog stand. I'd found a way to bypass police intervention, by trading on reclaimed private property for which I had a 35 year lease.

But strange things started to happen again. An empty mayonnaise bucket full of bagged silver coins disappeared from my bedroom. There was at least £1,000 in that bucket, but everything else in my house appeared to be untouched and there was no sign of a break-in. It was a mystery I was too busy to solve.

* * *

A few days later, the perforated platform was ready for collection and I decided to try out my new idea of selling hot dogs on private property that very night.

Using a table and my old two ring gas cooker I set myself up on the platform. I wasn't lit up and traded for an hour just to see what the Garda would do. It wasn't comfortable standing exposed on the platform, but a metal support bar, which ran from the building to the railing helped with my vertigo. The gardaí walked by and said nothing. Now I felt confident that my idea was going to work. I sold 60 hot dogs; exactly one pot full, and decided to call it a night.

Every weekend, the persistent psycho thug came to Leeson Street with his copycat hut, sat on the granite steps beside my restaurant and stared pure evil on the world until about 3.30 a.m. Then he went home, having made his screwed-up point.

But as soon as I was seen selling hot dogs from my table and chair set up on the platform, the idea was out. And it didn't take long for other interested parties to figure out the private property rule I was using to bypass police jurisdiction.

A week later, another man placed a fine looking hot dog stand on the wide granite steps of the building above Strings nightclub.

I got a phone call from one of the girls in my restaurant and drove in to check out this new addition to Leeson Street.

As far as I was concerned, things were going to change and I was delighted that I was going to be a part of this new reign of hot dog selling on the Street. My own stainless steel hot dog stand would be ready in a week's time. I parked my car near the entrance of The Hungry Wolf and was about to get out when I saw, in my rear view mirror, The General walk towards me with a demented expression upon his face.

I turned my head towards the passenger seat to avoid eye contact. To my surprise, and relief, The General walked past my car. He walked past my restaurant and then he stopped by the granite steps adjacent to it. He looked over at the other hot dog stand and remained motionless. He watched the crowds buy hot dogs and I watched him watch them.

Martin Cahill didn't move from his spot by the railing for 45 minutes. His expression was that of a bulldog watching a caged dog chew HIS bone. I stayed in my car with my hand near my face and watched the psycho perform his deathly stare. With so many odd people hanging around Leeson Street I don't think anybody noticed him standing there. Eventually The General turned and walked his heavy walk back up Leeson Street. Again I turned to pick up something invisible from the passenger floor. In my driver's side wing mirror I watched him get into a car and drive away.

I wondered if that was how he cast his reapers spell. I told the hot dog seller what I had seen and he seemed to take it with a brave pinch of salt.

'I'm just telling you what I saw,' I said.

'Thanks anyway,' he replied.

The next day, during the early hours of the morning, this vendor and his wife heard 'creepy people' noises around their home. The Garda were called, but the thugs had long gone. These noises were designed to frighten. The General feared no one, but the vendor's wife feared for her young child. Later that morning, his fine looking hot dog stand was burnt from its frame as it stood parked in a garage and that was the end of his hot dog career on Leeson Street.

* * *

A week later, on the first Thursday evening in June, my aluminium platform was slotted into position. I waited until 9 p.m. before I opened the new access gate in the railing and pushed the hot dog stand up a wooden ramp onto the platform. It was no man's time on Leeson Street—rush hour traffic over, late night trade not yet begun. The unit looked impressive as the halogen lights from the restaurant reflected against the polished stainless-steel surface. The way I saw it, this new hot dog stand was part of my restaurant with all its associated costs, it was my idea to sell hot dogs, my idea how to get around the Garda and I just didn't see how it was any of Martin Cahill's business.

At 11 p.m. I turned on the gas. Running the new hot dog stand would take a bit of getting used to, and now that I was exposed to the elements, the weather would take some getting used to as well. Less of a problem during the summer months; I would deal with the winter when my wrist bones began to crack the ketchup beat.

People stopped and looked at my stainless steel, rocket shaped hot dog stand. I felt like Neil Armstrong standing beside Apollo 11. Trade began. Hot dog production was slow—I would learn to speed up with practise and time. If my new venture proved to be successful it would add a great deal of value to my business. The gardaí walked by, looked at my set up and continued walking.

I heard later that the Garda Síochána had sought legal advice and were told there was nothing they could do to stop me from trading—not that they were ever that hell-bent on stopping me from selling hot dogs on Leeson Street. They were more interested in Cahill.

I finally had my licence to sell hot dogs on Leeson Street, and because I was now the only one selling hot dogs—the others had deemed it not worth the risk of upsetting The General—it got incredibly busy.

During a short lull I noticed that a big car had pulled up on the opposite side of the road. There were four mean looking men sitting inside the car and all of them were staring at me. With each passing minute my heartbeat gained momentum. I continued to serve the hungry.

Eventually, when my heart reached something like 140 beats per minute, the intimidating car drove away. I hadn't seen Mr Psycho Thug either, but then it was only Thursday night, and he only came on weekends.

Then, as occasionally happened on Leeson Street, the Garda did one of their pre-arranged raids. Within minutes the street was filled with disorientated bodies —it was the final rush of the night.

Standing on the platform all night long tired me even more than working inside the old hot dog stand

and packing it up took a lot longer as well. I rid the street of discarded kitchen towels, wheeled the new hot dog stand from the platform and attached it to the tow bar of my car. Finally, I took down the aluminium platform.

Once again I was shattered. The restaurant was coming into its element. It was in good hands with my two latest waitresses, two Protestant girls, looking after it.

'Have you never heard of The Protestant Work Ethic?' they once asked me when I complimented them on their swift waitressing skills.

I drove home slowly; unsure how well the narrow structure of the new hot dog stand would handle the road and then crawled a right turn onto Belmont Avenue. The street was silent as I pushed the steel rocket into my driveway. I opened the front door of my home and entered the hallway carrying the black plastic bag filled with the night's takings. I didn't even have the energy to make myself a cup of tea. I sat down on the black leather couch in the sitting room for a moment's contemplation. I thought about the four men I had seen.

What the hell did those mean looking men want? Staring over at me like that. They were hardly deliberating between a hot dog and breakfast at Manhattan's—for twenty minutes? It was the language of thugs. The 'You're fucking dead look' was very effective.

Suddenly I heard a noise; it was coming from the front of the house. My blood ran cold. I sprang up from the couch and ran across the room to the window. I stood on the glass coffee table, pulled the curtain to one side and looked out onto the street. Everything was parked and silent and then there was a loud crash. I fell to the floor but felt no pain. *What the fuck just happened?*

I looked around slightly dazed. The glass top of the coffee table was lying on two broken pieces of marble. I couldn't believe the glass had survived my weight, while the marble bass beneath it had cracked.

It was like getting a slap on my face. My imagination had played a wicked prank. I went to bed and lay awake for hours, my thoughts racing around as if they were in the Monte Carlo Grand Prix. Eventually exhaustion overruled and I fell into a deep slumber.

— CHAPTER NINE —

That morning, I woke up still dressed, stretched and made my way to the shower. Ten minutes of hot blissful solitude and then back to cold reality. A journey to the restaurant, phone calls for stock, and FAS interviews for two jobs already allocated.

The first guy was sitting at a table, coffee in hand, waiting for me. As he spoke to me his eyes never left the cigarette burn on the wooden table. He was a depressed ex-soldier who'd done some cooking in the army and was ready to give up on chefing altogether if this job didn't work out. *Don't they train these people at all in the art of interview?* He looked like he might poison us all, just to get even with a world that had treated him unfairly. Another guy with a jewellery shop of offensive piercings attached to most of his face and orange spiky hair told me not to mind how he looked, he did good work. I thought of my car parked on the double yellow lines outside the restaurant. The tickets were piling up in the glove compartment. After interviewing some of the most useless people in the city's workforce, I had an early lunch.

I don't think half of them wanted work, but FAS, the Employment Authority, had sent them, so they had to apply for the job in order to stay on welfare.

The reason I went through this rigmarole was because two staff members wouldn't get off the dole while they worked for me, and the authorities were cracking down on such practises by making employers responsible. So my two blackmarketeers officially joined my workforce via FAS and I paid them the extra £55 a week FAS would eventually pay me for employing them. At least they were signed off and I had one less problem to deal with.

After lunch I climbed the stairs to find a meter maid admiring my car. She was still at the examination stage so I called out to her and ran to the driver's side of my car. She seemed not to see or hear me and began to scribble into her docket book. I opened the door and got into my car, and then I started the engine. She kept writing, I reversed ten feet, she moved towards me still writing. I indicated right and drove away. In my rear view mirror I saw her stare in disbelief as she threw the folded parking ticket onto the street.

I drove to Eamon Dunphy's mews and asked him for his advice regarding The General. My mum and Eamon were no longer together, but we had always got on well.

'Ask them what they want and do exactly as they say. These are incredibly dangerous people,' he advised.

His advice was a real eye-opener. It had never occurred to me that burning out my hot dog stand as it stood impounded in the Garda Station had been a warning from The General for me never to trade hot dogs again. Thugs should write a pamphlet on terror-hints for the naïve.

It was too late for me to stop now. At 10 p.m., as I wheeled my new hot dog stand onto the perforated platform, I saw one of The General's men arrive in a van, with Cahill's yellow/orange hot dog hut in tow. I wondered if there was anything at all inside the hut. As he got out of his van I walked over to him.

'As you can see I've found a way to trade,' I said looking over at my new stand. He didn't reply. He turned away from me and unhooked the copy cat hut from his van.

'All I want to do is sell hot dogs in peace . . .'

'I'll get back to you in an hour,' he cut in.

The answer was short, the disdainful smirk gone. He climbed back into his van and drove away. I had recently learnt that Cahill hung around the Four Courts in his spare time, to learn how the law worked and how it could be toyed with. *Why couldn't The General get shot or arrested?* The rest of the rabble would fade like the sparks from an exploded firecracker.

On seeing such a display of arrogance, as he saw it, on what he now considered to be 'his turf', The General's evil gene went into overdrive. As far as I could see, I had infuriated him simply because I had come up with a way to get around the Garda with my hot dog stand before he could, and insisted on trying to earn a living. He knew nothing about protecting a business he had worked hard to establish. Whenever he needed to secure his business, it usually meant somebody got hurt. Unfortunately for me, the way he saw it, everything he saw was his business.

That night, one of The General's henchman came back to me and demanded two thirds of my gross takings. I traded that night because I was fully stocked to trade.

At 4 a.m. the thugs told me to finish up and it broke my heart when they took away my hard earned money, counted it out on a table in my restaurant and handed me back a paltry third, less the wage they paid the guy whose job it was to watch me. I also had to pay for ALL the stock. What was left wasn't worth the bitter insult of being one of The General's rodents.

The next day I told them that I couldn't continue on with such a humiliating arrangement, because my pride wouldn't allow it. I closed my space aged hot dog stand and never used it again.

They said that was fine by them; they had other plans anyway. I went home to bed, depressed and broken. I stayed awake for hours thinking about this repressive situation and decided that there was absolutely no way I could ever let myself become one of The General's minions. It was like being told I could have the cleaning job in my own company. Precious income was lost forever and my hot dog adventure was over.

I reckon I'd worked about a thousand nights on Leeson Street and eaten a good three thousand hot dogs with the works.

It has been suggested by some that the hot dog stands ruined Leeson Street; this couldn't be further from the truth. There were aspects of club dogma which were destructive to their own long term existence. The busty girl behind the counter would happily take your large paper denominated notes and hand you a bottle of plonk. Five minutes later a beefy bouncer might tell you to vacate the premises with absolutely no recall. Plonk stays, your money stays, you leave, and if you don't like it I will twist your arm behind your back and bash your head against the wall.

The hot dog stands had provided sustenance and character to the blood sucking night world of Leeson Street. They were an honest place of refuge, a place to chat and flirt. Their presence gave an added lease of life to a dying tradition that was Leeson Street.

* * *

It was two-thirty in the morning and I couldn't sleep. A week had passed since I'd sold my last hot dog and my body clock was all tangled up. I decided to get dressed and call into the restaurant.

The girl at the counter was surprised to see me. The restaurant was half full, which wasn't bad considering it was only a Tuesday night.

'Hi, I couldn't sleep,' I said and walked to the cash register. There's nothing like a cup of tea and a till full of notes to cheer me up.

'Oh, don't worry about that,' my waitress said, 'I'll be totting it up shortly.'

'That's okay; it'll give me something to do,' I replied.

I hit the readout button on the key pad and got a printout of the night's takings so far. The tiny typewriter tapped away obediently as I drank my tea. £286 minus £70 float equals £216. Not bad, considering there were still three hours of trade left. Next: count the money in the till to make sure it tallied with the receipt. This was more of a formality.

That's odd, I thought. There was £330 in the till. Initially I was chuffed, the takings were better again. But then I wondered how that was possible. *What was going on?* The girl had been sneaking glances in my direction the whole time. She wasn't happy that I'd called into the restaurant unexpectedly and she didn't want me near the cash register. What was she up to? It didn't make any sense to me—there was more money in the till than the printed readout, plus float, suggested there should be. I decided to hang around for the remainder of the shift. About a quarter of an hour later she asked if she could go home early because of period pains. As soon as she left, with her wages, I turned to the chef and asked his opinion.

'I don't know what she's up to, but she won't let anybody near that cash register and at the end of the night she takes all the money to one of those tables and counts it out,' he said.

Her takings were never as good as other staff working similar nights.

So I wasn't being paranoid. Up until now only the occasional 3kg bag of mozzarella or the odd bottle of wine had gone missing. Mozzarella was expensive, and I believe there were one or two Italian restaurants who might take a bag off your hands.

I figured out what she was doing. She wasn't typing every sale into the cash register and kept a mental note of the sum. Customers would be less concerned about getting a receipt in the early hours of the morning. At the end of her shift she pocketed the £60-£80 plus her wage and knew that when I checked the cash register, the numbers would tally.

* * *

A few days later I saw one of The General's men leave the building above my restaurant. This was an alarming development. *Please let there be some kind of rational explanation why this nasty little man had access to the building above my restaurant.* I drove to Killiney where my landlady lived in a big mansion. I rang the doorbell and was led into a kitchen the size of a gymnasium. This house once had many servants. Five minutes later the landlady arrived, and I got straight to the point, 'Who on earth have you rented the room above my restaurant to?' I asked.

'What do you mean?' she said, genuinely confused.

'I just saw a man, whom I happen to know is an associate of The General, step outside the front door of your building on Leeson Street...'

As it turned out my landlady had signed a two year, nine month lease for the room above my restaurant to an associate of the infamous General, who had used a pseudonym in his dealings with her. She hadn't known who she was dealing with or who he associated with. She would never have dealt with such people. My heart sank.

That weekend some stuck together shelves appeared on the wide granite steps above my restaurant and The General began selling hot dogs to the public. In the morning I had to clean up the ketchup smeared napkins around my restaurant if I wanted any lunch trade. Asking The General to clean up his own mess didn't seem like the smartest thing to do. But that victory wasn't enough for the scoundrel.

Business continued on tenterhooks during the quiet evening period, but wages and all the other fixed costs still needed paying. The landlady may have unintentionally let this undesirable person into the building, and the undesirable person may have been severely affecting my uninterrupted peaceful use of the basement, but the rent still had to be paid.

There was constant harassment from the floor above. As customers tried to enjoy their evening meal they were subjected to loud banging, which thundered above their heads. It sounded like two people were lifting a heavy desk and dropping it onto the floor.

This continued all evening. My mother, God bless her innocence, even called up to the apartment one evening and asked if they could move the furniture around a little more quietly.

The General had ordered his men to lift and drop tables all night long.

I was forced to close down the evening trade. I couldn't believe this was happening. Now I was left with lunches and late nights. You could make all the noise you wanted late at night; my customers wouldn't hear a thing. John Lee Hooker's 'Boom Boom Boom Boom', turned up at full volume, drowned out the terrorism from the room above.

My landlady wasn't happy about her newest tenant and began court proceedings to have the undesirable person evicted. Meanwhile, my overdraft was gaining weight, but I had an idea how I might slim it down.

* * *

I was no stranger to business ventures, having begun my first enterprise when I was 11 years old. As I rarely received pocket money, I raised the necessary capital by walking home from school to save the 2p bus fare, and supplemented this by asking the occasional sympathetic-looking adult for a loan of that same 2p bus fare. I found Bird Avenue the most lucrative stretch of road for raising funds. There you had time to analyse your prey as they approached—old ladies were best.

After three days I had saved the 18p I needed to buy a packet of tea cake mix from Quinnsworth Shopping Centre in Dundrum. (Ironically, The General had allegedly robbed the neighbouring Quinnsworth branch in Rathfarnham the previous year. Not that I had heard of him back then.)

At home I read the easy-mix instructions and baked 20 buns in the oven. Next day, during lunch break, I sold the buns for 3p each. I always sold out—for a while even the teachers were good customers, but eventually someone somewhere complained, and I was closed down.

* * *

I was standing outside my restaurant with a basket full of sandwiches hanging around my neck. Maybe The General would consider cold sandwiches a neutral product. What the hell did it have to do with him anyway?

My cap read 'The Sandwich Man' and my jumper offered 'Freshly made Sandwiches'.

Some people bought a sandwich and then there was a lull. I wasn't lit up or advertised. But I wasn't unseen either. This time I was approached by Pure Evil himself. It was The General.

— CHAPTER TEN —

'If you don't stop this bullshit you're dead,' The General said, and sliced his index finger suggestively across the Adam's apple of his short, fat neck. He stood not three feet from me, staring evil upon me, and his smell was awful; body odour must have been part of the intimidation.

'I'm just trying to make a living,' I said.

The General ignored my plea and walked back to sit down on the granite steps of the adjacent building. I stood paralysed. A hungry person approached and asked me what I was selling. I told him to go away. One of his henchmen sat next to his boss and looked over at me. There was no smile; he was probably informing his boss of my next move. For me, Leeson Street suddenly went silent. My eardrums were pulsating. A moment later I turned around and walked down the stairs. My heart was pounding wildly in a life threatening way, and my legs had turned to rubber. I could hardly keep myself from losing balance and falling over.

I pushed the front door, stepped into the lobby and locked the door behind me. I can't remember why my restaurant was closed that night.

What do I do now? I didn't want to go back outside. I walked into the restaurant, removed the sandwich basket from around my neck and put it onto a table. The empty restaurant had an air of naïve calm about it. This was my territory, but only just. *Beam me up Scotty.*

I looked up at Humphrey Bogart on one of the artistic plates hanging on the wall, next to him Captain Kirk was calling out for Spock. My mind was a jumble sale of thoughts. I picked up the basket and brought it into the kitchen where it was cooler. The sandwiches would be safe in there until the morning. I walked back to the front of the restaurant, stood still and looked up towards the footpath. Four legs were standing motionless behind the railing and not many people were walking past. There was no reason for anyone to be standing there. The nearest nightclub was at least four doors away. Two people were standing at the front of my restaurant . . . *waiting for me?* I didn't want to go back up those stairs, even if there were a lot of people—witnesses—on Leeson Street.

The superman plate stayed put. I put on my jacket and went into the kitchen and scanned the work counter and shelves. My mind was a terrified blank. At the back of the restaurant, beyond the car park, a dark laneway led to Pembroke Street. In the movies the audience would be telling me not to go out there. Leeson Street was bright with lots of people walking about, but this evil bastard was sitting on those granite steps orchestrating evil towards all he surveyed. A chef's knife lay on the steel preparation table. They would expect me to leave by the front door, I reasoned.

I grabbed the long sharp knife and crept out the back door. It was pitch black. I stood still and listened. Nothing, complete silence, the four-storey terraced building, which towered behind me, blanked out all sounds from the noisy main street. Slowly the walls and the ground came into focus.

What the hell was I doing with a kitchen knife in my hand?

I ran to the rear of the car park, peeked around the wall and ran the short distance along Pembroke Place onto Pembroke Street. I looked left and then right. A couple walked arm in arm and a hooker stood at her corner, looking eager and friendly. Everything seemed okay. No grim reapers of the night. I saw a taxi drive in my direction. The knife slid into my inside pocket and I put out my hand. Again I wondered what madness had prompted me to bring the knife. A professional thug would have taken it from me and sliced carpaccio from my hide. As the taxi turned left and drove up Leeson Street I covered my face with my hand. Through a gap in my fingers I saw two unpleasant large men standing at the entrance of my restaurant. They were two of the men that had stared the 'you're fucking dead look' at me weeks earlier from the intimidating big car. With bad people you can judge a book by its cover. They were not normal looking human beings. The lines on their faces, the furrow of their brows and the narrowness of their eyes had morphed their expressions into faces of evil from an early age. They were the human equivalent of dogs trained to kill.

The General was still sitting on the granite steps talking to his henchman, formulating his evil plans.

When I got home I sat in the downstairs sitting room and looked at the stars for several hours. I was safe for now—The General would assume that I was still inside my restaurant, but tomorrow would be different. *I have to stop standing up for my principles; it's going to give me a heart attack. This is not a movie and I am not Clint Eastwood.* The stars faded and were replaced by dawn.

I missed the good old days of selling hot dogs on a busy Saturday night to a bunch of friendly people having the craic. I missed the adrenalin rush, which enabled me to work at the speed of sound all through the night into the early morning. *Would the good old days ever return?* Finally exhaustion overruled and I fell asleep on the black leather couch.

Thoughts of my earlier encounter with The General played around in my head, and despite my fears, a smile spread across my lips. With a small sense of satisfaction, I recalled that sometimes, when I had to be, I could be more prepared than I looked.

When I was younger, maybe 11 or 12 years of age, I walked down the stairs of my father's house. Mrs Jones was sunbathing in the nude in her back garden. 'Wibble Wobbles' I used to call them. I continued on down into the hallway and opened the kitchen door. My father had glued a double bass bow and left it protruding precariously on a shelf by the kitchen door. The bow went flying through the air and snapped when it hit the floor. My father screamed at me and his hand instinctively shot down towards my face. My hands flew above my head in self-defence. He slammed the palm of his hand directly onto the sharp tip of the pencil I still held in my hand and then he screamed some more.

These instincts stayed with me. Fearing that I might be approached by The General, I had placed a tape recorder underneath the sandwiches I was selling. The General's threat to kill me had been recorded on tape. Next morning I called to Harcourt Street Garda Headquarters and gave the tape recording of The General threatening to kill.

Later that evening I gave the leftover sandwiches to a group of homeless people sleeping in a roofed car park near the back of the restaurant

I was worried to find that one of the national newspapers had printed a story on the situation regarding The General's activities on Leeson Street, naming me as a source. After several visits from a persistent journalist, I had eventually buckled and agreed to tell my version of events. Everything in it was true, but now I was a target of the infamous criminal.

Now I'm fucked.

The next day I called into Harcourt Terrace Garda Station to see how things were progressing regarding the evils of The General and putting a stop to his rot. I was told by the garda on hatch duty to go on through to the office at the back of the station. When I saw seven gardaí sitting around a large table drinking tea, joking, laughing, my spirits faded. It was three o'clock in the afternoon; hardly time for a tea break. I realised then that I was on my own.

* * *

The night was bustling. It was 25 November 1992. The popularity of my late night restaurant had exploded and I was back to working seven nights a week. I'd rid the restaurant of all inept employees and what remained was a dedicated and loyal staff.

There was a camp waiter, who announced one night before the start of business that as great as we all thought my Protestant girl Sarah was, 'I bet she can't suck cock as well as I can.' As so often seems to be the case with unthreatening gay men, he attracted a large number of female beauties into the restaurant. Local working class heroes, Mannix Flynn and Alan Devlin, often provided drink-induced, gravel-toned entertainment—Brutus stabbing Caesar kind of stuff—using the restaurant cutlery as props. Or Mannix might step onto a chair and recite unrefined poetry. The atmosphere in the restaurant was boisterous, healthy and exhilarating. Blues, jazz and music from the sixties played all night long and the money rolled in. 'White Rabbit', by Jefferson Airplane, was a personal favourite. I could ask Alice all night long.

Gradually people fell out of the restaurant and made their way up the stairs. One person even managed to rob a cane armchair from the waiting area in the lobby. The night came to an end at 7.30 a.m., the tills overflowed with money and the place was in turmoil. Chairs were overturned and some broken crockery lay on the floor. All part of a hectic, profitable night. Two girls walked into the restaurant looking for breakfast, or a drink. And a drink was what was needed by all. So *Damien*, who had worked the night with me, and I had drinks with the girls. Two hours later we all decided to go to my house.

'It's funny how the better looking one homed in on you when she found out you owned the place,' *Damien* said.

I had broken up with my girlfriend months earlier. The pressure of The General had taken its toll on me.

'Come on, your one isn't that bad,' I said.

The girls came back from the toilets and we made our way up the stairs to the street. I squeezed a bicycle belonging to one of the girls into the back of my car. With the buzz of the drink warming my mood on this Sunday morning, I remember seeing one of The General's men watching me as I drove away.

Once home we headed straight for the bedroom and a number of sins were committed before I and my early morning conquest fell asleep. When I woke up she wanted me to join her in the shower, but the refining properties of drink had worn off and I had a splitting headache. I went down the stairs, made a cup of tea; it made my head feel better and then I turned on the news. It was six o'clock in the evening. The phone rang.

'Mr Eulitz?'

'Yes.'

'I think you'd better come to Leeson Street, immediately.'

'Is everything okay?'

'Not exactly, your restaurant is on fire.'

I put on my shoes and drove into the city. The nightmare became a reality when I saw two fire engines parked outside my restaurant. I parked on the opposite side of the road and walked over. A fireman was returning a hose to his fire engine; another one was walking up the diagonal stairs. He looked exhausted. No one paid me any attention. I looked down into the basement. It was dark, wet and dreary. The fireman said it was okay for me to go down. When I stepped through the lobby into the dining area my heart sank. Water dripped from the ceiling, tables and chairs were overturned and charred, and everything was covered in a film of wet ash. The satirical plates that hung on the wall, running horizontally around the restaurant, were blistered and had lost all their natural colours. The closed zipper on Charlie Haughey's mouth was gone. The world war one biplane, which protruded from another plate now looked like it had crash-landed and the map of the world looked dark and unforgiving. Everything that was made of plastic—light covers, spoons, knives and forks stuck to the artistic plates—

was now shrunk and twisted into angry art. The blackboard hanging in the serving hatch still had Monday morning's food order written on it. It was a small sign of life. I looked around at the depressing sight and my heart fell further. *I hope those bastards rot in hell—I won't give up.*

The last fire brigade man left the basement and for a few minutes I stood alone and looked at the blackened corpse that had been my restaurant. I couldn't understand this senseless act of destruction.

Why? What purpose did any of this serve? They had their bloody hot dog thing up above. Why continue to attack me? As I looked around the desolation I felt my enthusiasm wane.

Those scummy little shits were here, pouring petrol, two hours ago, when my creation was still bright with colours. If only I could go back two hours in time.

I wish I'd been here with a gun—I'd shoot the bastards as they burrowed through the wooden door at the back of the restaurant. What good was this going to do him? He was a psychopath who needed to be put down.

I wished someone would shoot the evil bastard.

My staff arrived; we had a drink across the road in Darby O'Gills and then I had to let them all go. They didn't hold it against me.

Life came to a sudden halt. I went from all work and no play to no work and no pay. There was nothing for me to do except wait for the insurance money to re-build my restaurant.

One of my staff came to my home one day looking for some money, but I had none to give him, so I gave him a 2.5 kilogram tin of baked beans instead. He took the large tin and left.

The General has often been portrayed as a lovable rogue who made a mockery of the Garda, and while he did do that, he also directly caused hundreds of people to lose their jobs at a time when jobs were not that easy to come by in pre-Celtic Tiger Ireland. My staff now had to join the ranks of the unemployed, just like those at O'Connor's Jewellers whose business died the day The General's gang robbed it of nearly £2 million back in 1983, or the countless small shop owners he had terrorised into selling up, or shutting down.

The General set more buildings ablaze and the Garda did nothing to stop him. As far as they were concerned, he had lost his way and wasn't worth following around anymore. The way they saw it, his gang of the 1980s, the most ruthless in Ireland, had begun to fall apart. Maybe that was why he was picking on small fry like me.

They knew he was on Leeson Street every night, but since they had prevented him from running the hot dog business completely, they didn't seem to care what he did.

(A few high profile crimes in the following two years were to prove the Garda wrong on this assumption that The General was finished. He was instead forming a new generation of more ruthless gang members, treading water before planning another big robbery, involving the kidnapping of the chief executive of a bank.)

* * *

I'd been on The General's mind because I had continued to try to run my business and refused to pay him any more protection money. He'd probably seen the newspaper article citing me as a source too, and I guess he thought that by destroying my livelihood he would be killing two birds with the one stone.

The next evening I happened upon one of his henchmen. We got to chatting, if you could call it that.

'Why burn my restaurant?' I asked.

'To teach a lesson,' he replied.

The weeks passed by. I was alternating between two girlfriends, both of whom I'd recently become re-acquainted with and both of whom were showing a renewed interest in me. When I wasn't with either of them I was at home watching videos. In a bloke's sort of a way I wasn't going out with either of them. I went to Galway with one for a long weekend—to get away from it all. I think I deserved that. The girls probably thought the whole situation with The General was all very exciting, in the way some girls get turned on by danger, although one did ring up the house one day and say that she wanted to have a serious talk with the other to straighten things out.

The air in Galway was refreshing as only the blistery West can be. We stayed in a bed and breakfast and drank Guinness to live twiddely-diddley-dee music. On Monday morning we drove back to Dublin.

The insurance company was being slow on payment. Those advertisements, the ones showing houses getting damaged by whatever and the insurance company sorting it all out before you get home from your holidays, are not true. I wanted to repair my restaurant and get back to work. So I waited, went for walks and watched more videos.

But problems were mounting. I got a call from the health department.

'We've had complaints. The food in your restaurant is rotting away and the smell is attracting rats,' she said.

I didn't want to go back into that depressing basement, but it was still my responsibility. So I drove to the restaurant, put on a pair of extra tough black rubber gloves and walked down the stairs. The smell of rotting meat was unbearable as I entered the lobby. Not only was I looking for rotten meat to put into my black plastic bag, I was also looking out for any big fat rats who may already have laid claim to it. The finger print under a question mark plate lay shattered on the floor next to a charred chair. It felt spooky walking towards the kitchen at the back of the darkened restaurant. The sickly smell crept up my nose and I suddenly had an urge to vomit. The final assault on my olfactory senses came when I opened the door to the meat fridge. The electricity had been out for weeks. I nearly passed out. Even breathing through my mouth didn't seem to help. Gripping lumps of rotting meat was like picking up dead rats—or what I imagined it would be like picking up several dead rats. I put them into a plastic bag and retreated cautiously, ears and eyes wide open.

EAT: written using magazine cut out letters and varnished onto the backdrop of a dark green plate, hung on the wall by the door. The plate was now a message for vermin. A minute later I was walking up the stairs with the bag of rotten meat held at arms length. I put the bag into the boot of my car, careful not to puncture it, and began to drive home. On the way I saw a big yellow skip and decided to dump the bag of rotting meat into it. When I got home I had a long shower, watched a video and went to bed on my own.

Six hours later I heaved myself out of bed into a new day. I looked in the bathroom mirror as I peed. Dark rings circled my eyes and sprigs of hair gave a morning salute. A modelling job was out of the question. I threw some cold water across my face and went into the kitchen. I needed a strong mug of tea; one sugar, lots of milk. The first gulp was taken with closed eyes and my brain warmed up nicely. Armed with a mug of tea, I got into my car and headed back to the restaurant to meet with the health woman.

'Can I see documentary evidence of your disposal of the meat?' she asked.

'Excuse me?' I replied.

'I need to see evidence that you disposed of the meat in the correct manner.'

'It was rotten, disgusting and stank to high heaven. I dumped it in a skip on the way home.'

'Is it still there?'

'I have no idea. I can go and check if you like?'

'That won't be necessary Wolfgang, I believe you,' she said.

'Why did you need to see proof?' I asked because I was genuinely curious.

'You wouldn't believe it, but there's a market for old meat in Dublin city,' she said. I didn't pry any further.

* * *

I was still treading water. I didn't know what to do anymore, so I was beginning to lounge around, keeping a low profile. On 24 January 1993 I went to a Chinese restaurant in Blackrock for my 29th birthday. It was a quiet affair enjoyed with some friends. A couple of days later I was sitting at home watching television, but there was nothing worth watching. There rarely is unless you're willing to drop 50 points from your IQ.

A friend who was staying with me called Katja suggested I get a video and some milk for the morning. She went out with Jens, but was now on a break. She needed somewhere to stay, so I offered her a room in my house. *Damien* had moved out a couple of months earlier to pursue a career in art. It was purely platonic and we all stayed friends.

When I left the house it was already dark. There was a late January chill in the air, but thanks to the young Minister for the Environment, Mary Harney, no smog. I walked the short distance to the video library in the village and browsed the selection. There wasn't much left I hadn't already seen. I picked up *Johnny Young* and read the back-cover.

The movie was a futuristic thriller:

Seven-foot tall cryogenic-freezing modules are used by people for 'time absorption' linked with investment maturities, with only the expense of an electric current to maintain a life.

Then some parents begin using the human freezers as day-care centres for their children. The story revolves around a boy, who never grew up, having only lived two hours a day until his parents died of old age, seventy years after he was born.

That'll do for tonight; a future shittier than my own. I rented it out.

Half way home I remembered I'd forgotten to get milk and turned back towards the newsagents. I thought about calling into a friend's house nearby for a cup of tea and a chat, but I'd been calling into him and his girlfriend a lot recently and decided to give them a break. The road leading to my house was deserted. People were in their homes and curtains were drawn. I put the video under my arm and rummaged for my key.

Maybe I should just knock. I glanced over at the sitting room window. The curtains were fully drawn. More fully than I remembered, in that part of the brain where we remember these inconsequential little things. Katja must have done that; German precision to keep in the heat. The key slid into the lock but wouldn't turn, so I pulled it back a little and wiggled until all the pins fell into place. I pushed the door open and stepped into the hallway.

— CHAPTER ELEVEN —

As I lay tied up on the floor of my sitting room I wondered what in hell these evil people still wanted from me. The hot dog stand and the restaurant were burnt out. There was nothing left for them to take. What the hell did they want with Katja and I? Although I figured she was just in the wrong place at the wrong time.

I heard the crackle of walkie-talkie communication in the hall way. I didn't know what was going to happen. *Poor Katja, I bet she wishes now she'd stayed with Jens.* There was an extended silence . . .

The volume on the television was turned up. Once again I felt the solid barrel of a gun pushed against the back of my head. I was standing in the midst of purgatory.

But no question followed and then the gun was gone again. The psychological torture continued, conducted in a primitive form of English, using a limited combination of guttural sounds. And only the younger thug spoke.

A hand went into my other trouser pocket and something else was pulled out.

'What've you a dole card for?'

'I'm out of work.'

The thug laughed.

'You shouldn't be signing on,' he said.

You're questioning my morals. I was too upset to see the funny side of his warped hypocrisy.

I heard the gentle crackle of walkie-talkie communications in the hallway and the front door open and shut. Positions outside the house were being coordinated in whispers. A floor board creaked as one of the thugs stood near my head. I preferred it when they stood in the hallway. Something was unpleasantly familiar. It was that repugnant smell again; I couldn't believe he was standing over me. It was The General.

Was he making sure it was me? Did he want me to know that it was him?

Time passed by slowly and then, as if to break the monotony, a pillow was placed on the back of my head and I thought – *this is it.* I had resigned myself to that possibility; I couldn't get myself to embrace it as a certainty. My will to fight had evaporated. Memories of life raced, crashed and piled up inside my mind.

There was no spasm of a last second panic attack. No burst of energy to defend myself. My heart beat wildly and my thoughts were in chaos. I was drained of all strength, I hadn't the energy to lash out and my hands had gone numb from the tightness of the washing line cutting into my wrists.

I remembered the way in which a bounty hunter in a spaghetti western had used a pillow to silence the gunshot into his victim's tired old head. The volume on the television set was turned up even more. Now it was loud. My brain seized up. There were so many things I still wanted to do with my life; music, writing …

* * *

I'd come close to death before. When I was 13 my dad sent me onto the roof of his house in Kilgobbin Heights to paint the soffit, because the old paint was flaking. I positioned the ladder on our neighbour's flat garage roof and leaned it five feet across the open space to the edge of my dad's roof. While holding the paint pot in one hand, I began to climb the ladder, but the feet of the ladder began to slide backwards. I was half way across the open space and the grey solid pathway far below was making me dizzy. I had to make a quick decision keep going or turn back. The ladder sped up and I lurched forward to get to the roof before the top of the ladder slid down too far. The paint bucket fell 20 feet to the ground and white paint splattered everywhere. *Oh God, I'm going to get killed for this.*

The upper half of my body clung to the edge of the roof just as the ladder crashed to the ground. My legs had nothing to push against and dangled in the air.

'What the hell are you doing?' my father shouted.

The noise had disturbed him from his sunbathing.

'Help!' I answered.

'Christ, look at this mess.'

The friction of my body on the roof tiles was waning and I was beginning to slide backwards. If I fell to the ground from this height I would certainly be paralysed or die. My father climbed onto the garage roof, repositioned the ladder and pushed me back up onto the roof of his house, muttering.

The following year I was involved in an accident in Germany when my father's MG Midget was savaged by a juggernaut when the truck driver had fallen asleep at the wheel and driven into us. Miraculously, we both escaped alive, though I had to spend several weeks in hospital with a huge amount of stitches sticking out of the back of my head.

I wondered if there would be a miracle to save my life this time.

* * *

My life didn't flash before my eyes, because the pillow was moved from the back of my head to the back of my legs. In all this wickedness I felt a glimmer of hope. Only the television set filled the room with indistinguishable sound and then there was a loud bang. I felt nothing and believed the gunman had somehow missed his aim through the pillow. I let out a cry of pain to play along—could I be so lucky?

The tension was evaporating from my body. Then there was another loud shot. It felt as though someone had stabbed my lower leg with a hot knife. The pain was excruciating and I screamed out, but I also felt an unusual sense of relief, because I was still alive. I heard the front door slam shut.

Were they gone?

'Are they gone?' I asked in a painful whisper.

'I don't know, I think so,' Katja replied.

She freed herself and phoned the Garda. She came back into the sitting room and helped me to sit up. My leg was swollen and numb; it felt paralysed and heated up like a lump of molten lead. The thumping, stinging pain I was now experiencing seemed to be located at the back of my kneecap. *Would I be able to walk again?* I didn't have the strength to lift my leg. We waited for the ambulance to arrive. My hands were still tied behind my back; they were cold and numb. Katja went to the front door to make sure the ambulance found the right house. The pain in my leg intensified and I couldn't move it at all. It was as if my foot was glued to the floor.

Where the hell are those endorphins when you need them?

I looked across at the table. The lid of a game I'd invented lay beside the box. One of the picture cards was not in its compartment. That was not how I had left the board game. Maybe the Garda would get a fingerprint.

The Garda and the ambulance arrived simultaneously. My hands were untied and I was put on a stretcher. The joy of still being alive was now overshadowed by a growing anger of what had just happened.

'Do you know who did this to you?' a garda asked me.

'YOU KNOW DAMN WELL WHO DID THIS!!!'

Katja put her hand to my lips and told me to calm down and be careful what I said.

The ambulance siren went on and I was taken to nearby St Vincent's Hospital.

The journey was hazy. An injection took away some of the pain and some memory. All I wanted was to survive and leave the country. They could take everything. The whole ordeal had taken only an hour, from the moment I walked into the house to the agonising shot to the back of my leg, but I couldn't imagine getting over this any time soon. I just wanted out.

* * *

I lay on a trolley in a hallway of the hospital. A garda hovered around nearby, a nurse stood next to me and then my mother arrived. She was in and out of crying, trying to be brave. I don't remember much of what she said—I think she agreed that I should leave the country. I was wheeled somewhere, transferred onto a table, hooked up to wires; a needle with a small plastic tube was stuck into a vein on the back of my left hand. Blood flowed up the transparent tube, a small plastic knob was turned, the tube was removed and a needle was stuck into the plastic thing sticking out of the back of my left hand: I counted back from ten, nine, eight; the rest of the pain flowed out of my body and was replaced by warmth.

When I woke up there were seven other people lying in separate beds in a big colourless ward. I tried to move. A surge of pain tore through my lower leg as if someone was branding me with a hot iron. A nurse appeared and asked if I wanted something for the pain. I said yes. My leg was bandaged from scrotum to ankle and a large patch of dried blood covered much of it. I turned to one side and the nurse stuck a syringe in my bum cheek. I felt a little embarrassed, revealing my posterior like that, but I guess she'd seen more arses than I'd sold hot dogs.

The nurse told me to wiggle my toes. This would increase the blood circulation and speed up the drug's pain killing, euphoric effect.

Pethidine was good.

The feeling of well-being, warmth and relaxation, which now crept through my entire body made the world seem a better place. I now understood why people got hooked on drugs. Could you ever get bored of such a wonderful feeling?—a feeling derived from borrowing a little future happiness.

The bullet had cut diagonally through my calf muscle, crashed into my tibia bone and shattered, but it hadn't hit my kneecap, that must have been a nerve deception.

I was told by the sergeant dealing with my case that the gun had been angled into my leg to cause the maximum damage.

The sergeant told me of another gun shot victim who had died from lead blood poisoning. *Was this meant to make me feel better?* He suggested that the first shot I heard had been a blank bullet, put into the handgun to avoid accidental killing of a victim by a novice thug.

The Garda put a man on the door outside my ward; just like in the movies.

My two girlfriends came to visit me regularly, though at different times. They always phoned my mother before coming to the hospital. So this is what has to happen to get perfect harmony, when you're kind of seeing two birds at the same time.

The doctor unzipped my damaged calf from knee to ankle to fix the trauma inside my leg. The gardaí wanted the bullet, but the bullet was shrapnel.

After each operation my bandages needed regular changing. The back of my leg was slimy and sinewy and looked like a rotten piece of pink salmon with dried worms stuck to it. It was disgusting to look at. In between operations I received shots of pethidine at four hourly intervals.

A friend came to see me shortly after I got loaded up one day.

'I have to spend a fortune to get that stoned,' he said.

Every third day I was wheeled to the operating theatre for an operation on my leg. The view of

Georgian houses and trees through the large full length window was impressive. I was getting to like counting down from ten.

'We'll get you back in shape, so you can kick The General's ass,' my forthright doctor told me one afternoon and then the white liquid flowed into my vein and I was back with the fairies.

Eamon came to visit me with my mother one day. We talked a while and he asked me a lot of questions. I answered them as best I could.

Maybe the fact that I had recorded his threat to kill me meant The General could no longer kill me.

This was a comforting thought, and to some degree I could lie back and relax. Having a snooze after a shot of pethidine was always a good idea.

* * *

Breakfast in the hospital was served at 6.30 a.m. Why wake us so early? We had nothing else to do all day except lie in bed and wait for visitors. And the food wasn't that great. The human body needs wholesome food to repair itself. I was lucky, because my grandmother cooked fresh food for me every day and brought it to me in the ward.

During the day I read the Douglas Adams trilogy and at night I listened to classic David Bowie and 60s Rolling Stones on my walkman. The days passed by slowly and my leg muscles atrophied. The length of my leg now looked like a pale matchstick wrapped in bloodstained bandages. I pissed into a bedpan and one nurse said she saw my dick while I was under anaesthetic. She giggled. I remember she had crooked teeth and told me how much money she earned. My dignity was gone and I felt exposed, like a woman having a baby.

The police watch outside my ward ended when they were told there wouldn't be a bullet—the evidence was staying inside my leg, because to remove all the little bits of shrapnel would have damaged my leg even further, and perhaps prevented me from ever walking again.

Two male nurses came to get me. This would be the seventh operation.

A slice of skin was ripped from the inside of my upper left leg and grafted onto my open calf. They gave me morphine for that one. I was flying with the gods after the operation.

When the drug wore off the skin graft proved to be more painful than the gunshot wound had been.

A nurse came over and asked me if I was okay.

'My leg is throbbing,' I said.

'Hang on; I'll be right back with the medicine trolley.'

I asked the nurse how much pethidine she was giving me.

'50 mg; we were giving you 80 mg immediately after the operation.'

'Could you please reduce it to 20 mg?' I asked.

I was getting too fond of the 'white rabbit' and needed to clear my head.

The Garda came to the hospital. They wanted me to make a statement about everything that had happened to me, from the first moment I'd laid eyes on The General.

They told me that he had been in Rathmines Garda Station, two miles away from my home, at the exact moment I was shot, showing his vehicle insurance details. It was only a couple of minutes drive from my house to Rathmines Garda Station.

That was The General's way of claiming responsibility and pissing off the Garda at the same time—using the Garda station for his alibi. In fact I wondered why they didn't get suspicious whenever The General called in for trivial chit chat, and perhaps look in on any of his potential victims. I was reluctant to do or say anything that might restart this whole unpleasant affair.

'God forbid he should kill you. Alive, your words are only hearsay, but if he were to be successful and kill you, we can use your statement to charge him,' one of them said.

'And if he gets his hands on the statement, or someone tells him what's in the statement, he'll definitely kill me,' I said.

'The statement will be strictly confidential. Only the gardaí will ever know its contents. I give you my word.'

This man was high up in the Garda. You had to trust somebody.

A day earlier, TD Michael McDowell had paid me a fleeting visit and urged me to co-operate with the Garda. He was even higher up the chain of authority.

'Okay,' I said.

When I was finished telling the detectives everything I could tell them about The General and his wicked ways, they thanked me and said I'd done the right thing.

I was lying in bed and looking at my leg. My foot hung forward, limp, like an overly camp hand. The ligaments had shortened and tightened—to stand up straight on my damaged leg would have been impossible, like asking an ordinary person to do the splits.

One of the girlfriends massaged my foot and ankle as best she could but I knew there was a whole load of pain waiting for me when I got out of hospital.

A recently retired taxi man was dying on the other side of the ward. Nothing more could be done for him, so they kept him 'high' on drugs. The nurse told me it was the humane thing to do. During the night he would call out fares and pick-up places. He was back on the road and busy.

His family came to see him the next morning. They all stood around his bed in silence. A woman in her 30s, probably his daughter, began to cry. She could hardly control herself. It was very sad to see.

That night the taxi man sounded like a worn out radio and the following evening two orderlies wheeled him away, a blanket covering his face. It was macabre to see a dead man being wheeled out of the ward.

Despite everything that happened, I was determined not to let it stop me from living my life. I think I had taken the best attributes of my parents to heart—their ingenuity and resourcefulness—and hopefully left the rest behind.

When he was younger, my father was audacious and bright. He had studied music, but the totalitarian authorities expected him to work in a factory, which he had no intention of doing. 'How can people be expected to develop artistically if they are imprisoned in a mind-dulling factory all day long?' he argued. They took away his college privileges, so he went to West Berlin and got a scholarship there, just before the Wall went up. My mother was still trapped in East Berlin. My father was allowed to travel back and forth and always told the guards he was planning to leave the West for a much better life in East Germany, all the time checking out the security. He came up with the ingenious plan of strapping my mother underneath his high-axel Skoda and driving her out of East Germany. This was the one part of the vehicle border guards didn't seem to check.

My mother was seventeen years old when her horizontal body hovered across Checkpoint Charlie and the perilous no man's land into West Berlin. The journey took a lifetime. She went into hiding until her eighteenth birthday so as not to be deported back to East Germany for being a minor. It was an enormous act of courage for two people so very young.

* * *

I heard a man ask a little girl how old she was.

'Five,' the little girl replied.

'And when will you be six?' the man asked.

'When I'm finished being five,' the little girl replied.

Her mother smiled.

— CHAPTER TWELVE —

I'd been in hospital for 22 days and it was time for me to go home. I was nervous about going back into that house on Belmont Avenue, let alone sleeping in it all night long. One of the girls said she'd keep me company. As I hobbled out of the hospital on crutches, a bitter cold wind swished across my face. The hospital had felt secure, but now I was back in the real world and all the shit that came with it. Heaps of grey cumuli covered the sky, threatening to rain on the city. It was damp and already getting dark. The world outside was cold and windy, wet and dreary.

When I opened the front door of my home and stepped into the hallway I was overwhelmed with depression. The heart of my cave was cold and silent.

My girlfriend asked if I wanted a cup of tea—she'd had the good foresight to buy a fresh pint of milk. The house had been uninhabited for three weeks. I leaned on my walking stick and looked up at the darkening first floor hallway.

I could see the stocky gunman run down the stairs with his sawn off shotgun held steady in his hands and the other skinny thug point me into the sitting room with his hand gun. The process of putting this nightmare out of my mind would take a very long time.

'Yes, I'd love a cup.'

'Sure you're okay?'

'I'm fine, thanks.'

I limped into the sitting room and sat down on the couch where Katja had been tied up. Her experience had immediately earned her a room in Trinity College where she was studying. That was one way of getting a room in Trinity College.

She told me during a visit in hospital that the gangsters hadn't found the £700 college fees she'd hidden in her bedroom.

'You had £700 in your bedroom, the whole time?' I asked incredulously.

* * *

A few red bloodstains lay on the grey carpet as a painful reminder of what had happened. It's strange how such a small mark could symbolise so much damage and psychological upheaval. The house had been un-lived in for three weeks and smelt musty. The presence of dogs, cats, ashtrays, old brick and a touch of damp, all absorbed by wall to wall carpeting over many years, was nasally traumatic after three weeks in an antiseptically cleaned hospital.

My tea arrived and we sat down next to the bloodstain. She looked at the floor.

'Is this where you were shot?' she said pointing to the bloodstained carpet. The word 'shot' sent a shudder through my entire body.

'I don't want to talk about it.'

My words came fast and rude; I didn't want to relive the experience in any way by talking about what had happened to me.

She immediately understood that perhaps there were some questions which shouldn't be asked. That line of morbid curiosity could wait.

'Okay, do you want to watch television?' she asked.

'I need to bring back the video, it's three weeks overdue,' I replied.

'Do you want me to bring it back for you?'

'We can both do it, I need the exercise,' I said.

'Do you want to do it now?'

'Might as well.'

'I assume you didn't get to watch it, of course not, I'm sorry, I didn't mean . . .'

The poor girl wasn't sure what she could say now without upsetting me.

'It's okay. Do you want to turn on the gas fire? At least the place will be warm when we get back,' I said.

In order to light the coal effect fire you had to bend down to the ground and push a knob. Sore if I tried, so she obliged.

I couldn't bring myself to watch the video we were returning. It was the video I had taken out the night I was shot and to watch it now would have brought back traumatic memories. Thoughts of what I did wrong on my approach to the house, how I might have avoided the gunman, tackled him, somehow got into the sitting room and yanked the couch, with Katja on it, across the floor and up against the door—and then some more furniture against the couch—and screamed. What I should have done when I first felt something was wrong in the hallway. It's strange how the mind works when it's travelling down a cul-de-sac of torment.

The friendly oboe player I'd once worked with in the RTÉ Symphony Orchestra, now turned video movie dispenser, wouldn't even hear of an apology for the late film. I guess I'd had my 15 minutes of pain.

We decided to look around for another film. I picked one up and read the back cover:

The final days of World War Two.
From a secure region of the Bavarian Alps an untested German prototype V3 two-stage rocket blasts into the atmosphere, carrying a single two-tonne nuclear warhead. It too is untested and is the only one in existence. With the bluff of many more to come, this was to be Hitler's last stand. Hours later, the missile disappears from radar and the following day, as Russian tanks and mortars pound his underground bunker, the once powerful dictator commits suicide.
In the early hours of 29 April, 1945 some residents of New York see a bright flare in the sky. Then the flame disappears.
Present Day: suddenly and without warning the Nazi Cruise Missile reappears two hundred miles above New York City, travelling at four thousand miles per hour. Panic on the ground spreads like a virus as the glow in

the pre-dawn sky grows steadily brighter. Heartbeats race with a hopeless foreboding. Orders are rushed to get fighter jets airborne and frantic efforts are made to contact German authorities for assistance . . .

At the counter David asked me how I was. I said I was fine, considering. He said not to worry about the rent on the old video and handed me my new video. I said the chances of getting shot again, tonight, were slim.

I took the video; *Hitler's Last Stand* and we left the shop.

There were a few cautious hellos from strolling neighbours as I hobbled back to the house, my girlfriend by my side all the way.

At 11.00 p.m. we decided to go to bed. There was only one pillow by the head board.

'Police must have the other one for evidence and I don't think I want it back either.'

'Was that the pillow they used for . . . ?'

I looked at her and exhaled. She understood immediately. It took me quite a while to get undressed. Removing my trousers was like peeling a plaster from a tender wound. She helped in the end. The dried patch of darkened red/purple blood on the white bandage around my leg looked revolting to me. Despite my lack of sex-appeal we got into bed and we cuddled up; her voluptuous naked body moulding around my torso.

'I'm glad I wasn't here the night it happened,' she said.

'What, three weeks ago?' I asked.

'Yes.'

'Well that's understandable.'

'No, I mean I'd be mortified if we'd been found tied up in bed by the police and my parents found out we were sleeping together.'

'You are hilarious. You're more concerned about what your parents would think if you were found tied up in bed with me, than the danger of nearly getting killed.'

'They take sin very seriously.'

We talked some more and she was first to fall asleep. It felt reassuring having her body next to mine.

When I woke up she was still fast asleep and pressed up against my body. I lay still and let my mind wander. But there was nowhere good for it to go.

The experience of being tied up, humiliated and shot by these human vermin would haunt me for years to come. I was an angry man and there was little I could do about it.

Lying in bed at night I thought of how I would kill The General, though every time I had him in my vivid, imaginary sights, I found it impossible to pull the trigger—as if my own morality held me back. The fact that I was a better man than him was scant consolation.

The following night I was alone. I was apprehensive and jumpy. Last night the bad guys still thought I was in hospital; tonight they'd know I was out. I had absolutely nothing left for Martin Cahill to take from me, except of course my life, and I wondered if that was the next step in his vicious campaign against me. A worried mind can play wicked games with one's sanity. I barricaded myself into my bedroom by angling the back of a chair under the door handle and pushing my desk against the chair. I went to bed but found myself staring at the ceiling, flinching at every little noise I heard or thought I heard. A friend had given me a hurley stick and it now stood leaning against the wall next to my bed. A million thoughts raced through my mind. What was I going to do now? How was I going to survive? I didn't have any skills to speak of. These inhumane thugs would stop at nothing to prevent me from making a decent living, just to teach others who dared to disobey. They operated in tandem with the media and those vultures were only interested in a story that sold. Pain and misery sold.

I stared out of the bedroom window. The moon and the stars reflected light on the backs of cloud formations, revealing faint outlines of what looked like moving nebula. A large black spider clung patiently to the inside of the window. Three flies were trapped in its web and still alive. They struggled to free themselves and the spider waited. One by one the flies grew tired, their little hair-like legs not able for such a powerful trap. With their destiny a foregone conclusion, the flies surrendered unconditionally and the hungry spider moved in for the kill.

I reflected on the belief that a spider brings good luck before midnight and bad luck after. I returned to the relative darkness of the room. Then, as my heartbeat slowed to a steady 58 beats a minute, I fell asleep, and dreamed of days gone by.

* * *

I called to Vergemount Hall to claim disability benefit. The room was full of young single mothers claiming unmarried mother's allowance. Some of them looked fabulous and were now a little wiser than their peers. Pregnancy can bring out the full voluptuous beauty of a woman. After an hour's fantasizing, I was called into the office. The woman behind the counter asked me if I was living alone. I told her that I was. More questions were asked and I explained my tale of woe. The woman said that she'd be in touch with me. She didn't seem friendly at all.

Some days later I phoned to ask about my claim.

'I am having a problem with your claim,' she said.

'What kind of a problem?' I asked.

'You told me you were living alone.'

'I am.'

'Well I read in the newspaper that your girlfriend was tied up with you when you were shot.'

Her response came as quite a shock to me.

'Well for your information that girl was only a friend of mine and she's since moved out. You can take an educated guess why.'

'I'm going to have to inspect the premises . . .'

'Don't bother; I'll sort out something else.'

I hung up. I was furious that this woman, employed by the state to help people, should so callously suggest my claim was invalid based on an article she read in a newspaper.

The loss adjuster of the insurance company phoned and asked to see me.

I entered the plush building situated on the corner of Fitzwilliam Square and hobbled into an opulent room. The loss adjuster asked me to sit down. He was young, sparkish and didn't waste any time.

The insurance company was not going to honour their agreement because of an immaterial flaw with the paperwork. These were not his words, but that was what he meant. There would be no insurance money to rebuild my restaurant. An employee of the company had filled out the insurance application form in great haste and I had signed it without proper thought. I could tell the loss adjuster felt guilty as hell as I stood up and hobbled out of the office.

'I'm very sorry about this,' he said.

I fought them with words on paper. I didn't have the money to fight them with people in court.

Within a few determined days I was walking again, without the aid of crutches, but with the aid of Solpadeine. Taking a couple of Solbs and walking along Sandymount beach stretched my tightened ligaments and soon the limp was gone.

In March 1993 I walked into the dole office on Tara Street and told them I was fit for work and that I wanted to sign back on. The pain in my leg grew unbearable as I stood in line. That seemed to be my worst discomfort; standing in one position for any length of time. The calf of my leg heated up until it throbbed with intolerable pain and felt like it was going to explode.

In the welfare office standing in line was a pastime. Maybe they thought you'd eventually tire and get a job. When I got to the counter the girl looked at my file and said 'don't worry love'. I was signed on.

The General had once shot one of her colleagues for cutting off his welfare payments. I remembered reading about it in the paper. The man had been kidnapped in front of his wife and young children, driven to south Dublin and shot in both thighs. He had signed a form cutting off The General's dole. In other words, he was doing his job. Something Martin Cahill knew nothing about.

I called into the main FAS office in the city to collect money owed to me from the employment scheme I had participated in.

I was looking for £1,100—11 weeks back payment for my two FAS workers; my calculations were accurate. The civil servant came out of his office with a form for me to sign. I noticed the figure of £1,400 on it. I pointed out that the amount should only be £1,100, as the restaurant was now closed and the two lads had only been employed nine and 11 weeks respectably.

'So you're not open now?'

'Well no, the restaurant was burnt out.'

'So these two men are no longer in your employment?'

'I only had the one restaurant, and it's been burnt out; nobody's working there.'

'Well then I can't give you any money.'

'Why not? I asked. 'These men did work for me nine and 11 weeks continually and I have already paid all their taxes,' I explained.

'Yes, but the scheme requires that they stay employed for the full year or it invalidates the contract.'

'Excuse me; it's not my fault my restaurant was burnt out by gangsters.'

'I realise that, but I have to follow the rules.'

'I need this money badly.'

'There's nothing I can do about it.'

'But I've already paid both men the money you're meant to be giving me now. I'm just claiming it back, as agreed when I employed them in the first place.'

'I'm sorry, but there is nothing I can do for you.'

'You were about to hand me a cheque for £1,400.'

'I'm sorry but I'm responsible to Brussels.'

'You've got to be kidding, if I hadn't said anything, I'd be walking out of here with a cheque for £1400 in my pocket.'

'You would eventually have had to pay the money back.'

'I can't believe this.'

I shook my head and walked away. Honesty doesn't always pay. It had started to rain. March can be bitterly cold in Dublin. My leg was throbbing with pain, even when I walked, so I did something I rarely do. I hailed a taxi.

'Where to head?'

'Donnybrook please.'

The taxi man pressed buttons on his meter and engaged first gear. I watched people go about their daily business. I wanted to be any one of them as one envies a cat sleeping in the sunshine corner of a room. I afforded myself a smile. A corporation employee, walking at a leisurely pace, blew litter from the footpath using his petrol-driven leaf blower. A light breeze whirled the loose papers around his body and they settled on the footpath behind him.

The taxi man spoke uninterrupted of the faltering economy. The tip of his grey goatee bobbed as if tapping out a message in Morse code.

'You know the good times are coming to an end when smiling clean-shaven men wearing pressed white shirts and strong pungent aftershave start selling you their religion door to door.'

'They haven't called to me yet,' I replied.

'Isn't it funny how the word, 'devalue' is underneath the word "Deutschmark" in the *Oxford English Mini Dictionary?*' he said.

My great grandfather had lost everything in the hyperinflation which devastated Germany in the early twenties. He had saved paper money his entire life until one day it had turned back into paper.

'That's kind of ironic alright,' I answered.

'Have you ever been to an auction?' he asked.

'Once; why?'

'Did you ever notice that just when the bidding starts you get an itchy head?'

The radio went on:

'In Dublin circuit court today a man received a six-month prison sentence for passing counterfeit money. The court heard that a Mr Reynolds had used the £900 to pay an English prostitute for an extravagant evening's entertainment . . .

'Can't imagine she'd be able to claim the money back either,' the taxi man said.

'I think she'll be alright,' I said.

The taxi man stopped at the bottom of Belmont Avenue and I gave him a paper ten. It's funny how long it takes taxi men to find the last bit of change they owe you.

'Do you mind if I owe you 30 pence?' the taxi man asked as he looked through an empty pouch.

* * *

In April the leasing company wanted their money for the restaurant equipment. The letters of request had changed colour from white to a blood red and now they threatened court action. I was no longer a financial target for them so they went after my mother who had gone as guarantor for the financing loan. The bank was incredibly ruthless.

My mother was scared, borrowed money, and made a deal with them. It was around the same time the big bank was letting some politicians away with millions in bad debt. Only the little guy gets to feel the soles of their black boots.

Although I had asked my bank to freeze my account they continued to pay direct debits. Within a week my overdraft exploded as the vultures dived in. Most of the payments were for stock and equipment now destroyed. The telephone company cut me off at home, because the restaurant phone bill wasn't paid. Now my alarm system didn't work. They didn't tell me that could happen when I signed up. And this was the one time in my life that I really needed the comfort of a house alarm.

***

Some time in May there was a knock on the door. I was very cautious about opening my front door these days. I looked through the little spy-hole *Damien* had installed for me before he left to pursue a career in art. Installing spy holes in people's front doors had been one of his many talked-to-death ideas.

It was the friendly garda sergeant who had been dealing with my case. I opened the door. He had a bit of bad news and didn't quite know how to tell me. I invited him into the house and we went into the kitchen. I made tea for us both.

'Those fines have come back to haunt you,' he said.

I had £1,200 worth of parking fines and £1,000 worth of hot dog stand health fines the gardaí tried to make go away after my troubles.

'What do you mean?' I asked.

'That damned Brendan Smyth . . .'

'What has a child molesting priest got to do with unpaid fines?'

The paedophile priest, whose summonses had also been brushed under the table for a very long time, was now being held accountable for his disgusting actions. Someone had had enough of the cover-ups. Old summonses re-surfaced like relatives at the reading of a lucrative will.

'I'm sorry, there's nothing I can do about this,' he said.

'Neither can I,' I replied.

'I've made a deal with Mountjoy Prison. They'll keep you inside for 30 days plus you pay a £400 fine,' he said.

'No way: I get shot and lose everything I worked for. The General gets away with it, rides around in a brand new Mercedes, eats in the best restaurants and I'm the one who goes to prison with a fine. What kind of a deal is that? I'll go to the papers; they'd love a story like that,' I said.

'Okay Wolfie, leave it with me. So how are things anyway . . . ?'

The next day he returned. I was painting an outside window frame. He seemed a little excited.

'I've got them down to 15 days and a £250 fine.'

'I haven't got any money,' I replied.

By the fourth day I was sanding the downstairs sitting room floor and he was down to 15 days, but I would only serve one day because of prison overcrowding, and there would be no fine.

'Okay, I'll do it.'

'But whatever you do don't let them send you to an open prison, or you'll have to serve the whole 15 days.'

'Gotcha,' I replied.

A couple of days later a garda car came by the house to collect me. My new girlfriend waved from an upstairs window as I got into the unmarked car. It was a wet miserable journey from Donnybrook to Mountjoy prison. *What a waste of manpower—Dublin was really going to be a safer place with me out of the game for 24 hours.*

We drove through the big iron 'King Kong' gates of the prison and I was handed over to one of the screws. I went through the induction process of stripping down, putting on prison clothes and getting my bed pack.

'You want to be considered for an open prison?'

'No.'

'You a homosexual?'

'No.'

I had my own cell and an hour to myself before a loud double clank and the metal door opened up.

'Association' said the institutionalised voice of a screw.

I stepped outside my cell into an open-plan concrete 'Oz'. The '15 days' written on my identification card by the door was startling to see. I really hoped these guys hadn't forgotten the deal. The place was dust free and freshly cleaned, but smelt of monotonous repression.

I had a game of chess with a lifer, who after 15 years of 'Bird', was soon to be released back into society. He told me he had three grown up children who all lived in England. He himself was hoping to live in Scotland, but as yet, had nowhere to stay. I asked if his children would help him out. He told me that they didn't like him. He then explained that they didn't like him because he had killed their mother. I reluctantly said, 'Check mate'.

He told me I took too long between moves. He was right.

Lock up came at 10 p.m. and the prison went to sleep. In the morning the same screw from the night before clanked the door open (that was some overtime he had clocked up) and another one shouted, 'BREAKFAST!'

Cornflakes, toast, eggs, sausages and beans. The food wasn't that bad, considering it was prison.

'Eulitz! Get your bed pack folded and come with me!'

I did as he shouted, saying good-bye to some of the lads as I left the prison wing. There were 12 people released that morning. I got talking to one of them. He had served a night for £3,000 worth of fines. It was certainly worth doing a night in prison for that kind of money.

'Anybody collecting you?' shouted the screw.

'No.'

'Got any money for transport?'

'No.'

'Okay, here's £5. Sign here. You're on a 14-day licence. Stay out of trouble.'

'Yes.'

It was still raining when I got on the bus for the city centre and then another one for home. My garden shed had been delivered and erected.

* * *

It irked me when I later discovered that the Gardaí knew a man had been watching my home days before I was shot. A neighbour had seen the long haired youth stare up at my bedroom from a nearby laneway. The neighbour phoned the Gardaí, but just as their squad car arrived the nimble rat scaled a wall, light as a feather, into the schoolyard behind my home and disappeared. Rather than inform me of what had happened, warn me that I was still at risk, the Gardaí kept me in the dark.

If they had warned me that a man was seen watching my home I would have left the country for a couple of months. That really angered me.

And I was annoyed with myself because I had handed The General my idea on a silver platter—trading on private property. And for that lucrative idea, and all that followed on from it, the idiot shot me. His lackeys continued selling hot dogs from the wooden shelf unit

—neither the Health authorities nor the Garda went near him.

*   *   *

Soon after, I was sitting in front of the Criminal Injuries Tribunal. The three people behind their desks sympathised with my ordeal but told me I wouldn't be entitled to any compensation. *If I had a dollar for every time someone sympathised with my ordeal . . .*

They informed me that since 1986, the state no longer gave compensation for the pain and suffering caused by an act of organised crime such as I had suffered and that, in relation to loss of earnings, at the time of the incident I wasn't earning a wage.

The letter I received from the criminal injuries compensation tribunal explained:

'The applicant's claim for loss of earnings is based on the premise that he was unable to run his restaurant. His restaurant premises had however, been destroyed by fire in November 1992. It appears that this was a malicious act and, probably, perpetrated by the same person or persons who injured him in January 1993. The Applicant was drawing unemployment benefit at the time that he sustained personal injuries. The compensation scheme which this tribunal operates only relates to loss which arises from personal injury which is directly attributable to a crime of violence. It does not relate to loss attributable to a crime of violence unless personal injury is involved. The crime which deprived the Applicant of his livelihood was the burning down of his restaurant in 1992. That did not involve personal injury to the Applicant. The tribunal is, accordingly, unable to award the Applicant any sum in respect of the loss of earnings which he claims.'

I sighed away my ambitions. *This is the stuff of unrealistic movies.* If I'd been shot before my restaurant was destroyed, I'd have been entitled to some compensation.

I was ostracised by the insurance world, unable to insure my home, let alone another business venture. Eventually a staff member of one large insurance firm told me, in confidence, the true reason I was being blanked by all insurance companies—I was considered high risk.

As the victim I was now being victimised.

I started to wonder if Dublin was really a good place to live anymore. A black fellow I recognised from Leeson Street walked past my home one day.

'Hello my friend,' he said.

'Hello, how are you?' I replied.

'Not bad, not bad,' he admitted.

'You must be a doctor by now?'

'Yes, well actually I am going back to Nigeria,' he said.

'Why? Surely you would do well here.'

'My friend; you were shot in this country, and you are white.'

He had a point.

After careful consideration I decided against re-opening my restaurant. Life was too short. In July, 1993 I sold the 35 year lease to a chef who had worked in Strings nightclub, and my connection with Leeson Street was severed permanently.

I called into the restaurant one last time, days before it was due to re-open. I found the experience incredibly upsetting. The restaurant I had built was in the hands of another and there was nothing I could do about it. The pain of that reality burnt me from within as I stood in the dining area, and with all of my limbs trembling I couldn't wait to get out of that basement.

I retreated into the safety of my own home, because there is a limit to how far a person can fall before hitting something. Buying a DIY manual and following its simple instructions broke my fall. Renovating my home was my chosen therapy. No one would bother me there.

I bought a long haired German Shepherd dog I called Heidi and stopped barricading my bedroom door at night. I felt safe for the first time in quite a while, and decided to take a break from my ambitions. I went on the razz with a recently acquainted, similarly minded group of lads. I took in tenants and they funded my new experience.

I discovered Dublin's beer drinking culture. Dublin was a great place to be if you had spending money and time to nurse a hangover in the morning. A steady income from my tenants' rent meant that I had both. The economic boom had just begun, but had yet to be named. The nightlife was full of twenty-something-year-old girls looking for fun and no complications.

The church had been telling girls to live by one set of rules; instinct was now pulling them in the other direction, and a little of it trickled my way.

I was out of the business I had worked so hard to establish, but I was now free to do what I wanted. I started to forget all about The General and his twisted mindset. I read in the papers that he was becoming more and more erratic, getting involved in small things that really shouldn't have bothered him, even more so than when he decided to pick on me.

I guessed it was only a matter of time before he got his comeuppance and picked a fight with the wrong group of people. He had chosen to live as a criminal, never doing an honest day's work, and he'd gained a lot through his ruthlessness, but in the end he was living on borrowed time. As for me; I had lost a lot, but at least I was still alive.

— EPILOGUE —

On the afternoon of 18 August 1994, a man wearing a corporation uniform motioned a car to slow down at a T-junction in Ranelagh. Few would have been able to identify the driver of the car, but this man knew exactly who he was. Without compunction the man emptied the magazine of his handgun into the driver as if filling a pin cushion. Still in gear, the car stumbled forwards and crashed into a lamppost on the opposite side of the road. The bully, who thought he was invincible, was dead.

His assailant jumped onto the back of a motorbike and was sped away by an accomplice. A few hours later the IRA and INLA squabbled over the bragging rights to his murder.

Less than a mile away, paintbrush in hand, I heard over the radio the words that immediately grabbed my attention: 'Dublin crime boss Martin Cahill, known as The General, has been gunned down in his car in Ranelagh.'

I wiped the paintbrush on the rim of the paint can and laid it down across the top. I began to creep towards the radio, so as not to miss out on a single word.

A painter I had employed to help me renovate my house stopped what he was doing and also listened to the news.

'I'm glad you're here,' I said.

'Why do you say that?' he asked.

'Because you're my alibi.'

It felt like a burden had been lifted from my shoulders—this would help relieve some of the anger I had been living with. I finally had closure on my nightmare. I did find myself thinking, *what an awful way to go—hunched over a steering wheel, riddled with bullets—you wouldn't wish that on your worst enemy.*

* * *

In the end, Martin Cahill's killers had been able to do a dry run of their attack in the days leading up to his shooting because his actions had become so predictable. He left his house at the same time every day, rounding off every day in the same restaurant before heading to Leeson Street to intimidate more people. He could no longer trust a loyal bodyguard, so for the first time in many years he sometimes had to venture out alone. At the height of his power he had huge influence and commanded a loyal gang, but he was never liked, and when news of his death came through, few people mourned. On the contrary, many in Dublin celebrated that night, as did I.

* * *

Two weeks later there was a knock on my front door. I looked through the spy hole—old habits die hard— and saw three gardaí standing in the porch. I opened the door cautiously, and they asked if they could come in.

'You probably know why we're here,' one of them said.

'I can guess,' I replied.

I led them upstairs to the sitting room and we all sat down. They got straight to the point.

'Did you kill Martin Cahill?'

I laughed.

'No.'

'Did you employ someone to kill Martin Cahill?'

'No.'

Where were you on the afternoon of 18 August?'

'I was here in the house painting, all day.'

'Can anyone else confirm this?'

'Yes, the other guy who was painting with me.'

'Okay. Do you know who killed Martin Cahill?'

'No.'

And there the interrogation ended. They all had a laugh about what happened to The General, and then asked me how my leg was, before they went on their way.

Using all the rent I was now collecting, I put down a £2,000 booking deposit on another house and told my solicitor to delay the contracts until I had the next £3,000 saved to make up the deposit. The bank gave me a loan to make up the remaining £50,000 I needed to buy the small cottage on Portobello Road. A year later, with my bank now more eager than before to lend me money, I bought a third house nearby. Soon after that, the property market began to soar. I was sitting on a new goldmine . . . I was back in business.

— THE PERFECT HOT DOG—

The six-inch bread roll should be fresh, look like the model of an airship and have an incredibly light consistency. Sliced open from end to end and toasted on both sides, a five-inch pork frankfurter, boiled for no more than five to ten minutes, is placed into the opening of the bread roll. A three millimetre line of Heinz ketchup and two millimetre line of mild mustard is squirted along either side of the frankfurter where it touches the bread. Finally a fork load of freshly made coleslaw is laid along the top of the frankfurter. When the customer bites into the hot dog he or she will experience the immediate sensation of a crispy warm bread roll, the pop of a hot tasty frankfurter, mixed sauces and cold coleslaw all at once. Such a lightweight, scrumptious experience will not seriously quench the customer's appetite; it will however, excite the customer's palate into demanding a repeat experience. After all, they were only £1 each.

WELCOME TO HELL
ONE MAN'S FIGHT FOR LIFE INSIDE THE BANGKOK HILTON
by Colin Martin

Written from his cell and smuggled out page by page, Colin Martin's autobiography chronicles an innocent man's struggle to survive inside one of the world's most dangerous prisons.

After being swindled out of a fortune, Martin was let down by the hopelessly corrupt Thai police. Forced to rely upon his own resources, he tracked down the man who conned him and, drawn into a fight, accidentally stabbed and killed that man's bodyguard.

Martin was arrested, denied a fair trial, convicted of murder and thrown into prison—where he remained for eight years.

Honest and often disturbing—but told with a surprising humour—Welcome to Hell is the remarkable story of how Martin was denied justice again and again.

In his extraordinary account, he describes the swindle, his arrest and vicious torture by police, the unfair trial, and the eight years of brutality and squalor he was forced to endure.

SURVIVOR

MEMOIRS OF A PROSTITUTE

by Martina Keogh

with Jean Harrington

Survivor is the true story of a woman who started in prostitution when she was just 8 years old. Martina Keogh progressed from a brothel on Benburb Street to sporadic bouts of prostitution in St. Stephen's Green and the Phoenix Park.

When Martina was 15 she moved to the red-light district of Dublin where she sold her body for more than 30 years. This book details the problems the prostitute encounters with the police, the pimps, the punters and the public. It horrifies the reader as it reveals the violence she suffered on the streets: the weekly rapes, beatings and attempted murders.

Survivor reveals for the first time how prostitution works; the money involved, the seediness, the glamour and the good times.